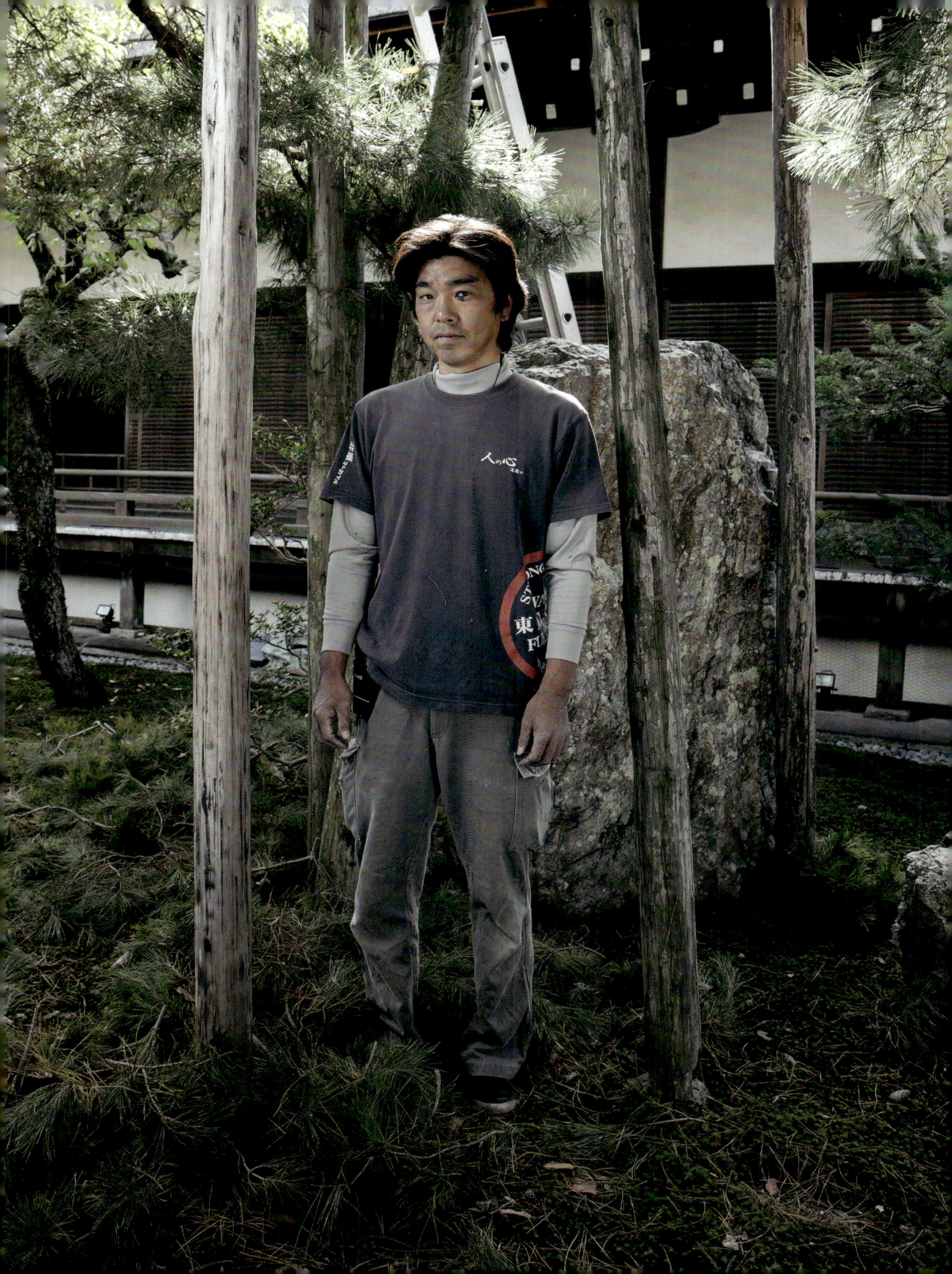
人の心

EXIT STRA TE GIES

black dog publishing
london uk

Contents

Ritual

Sacrifice

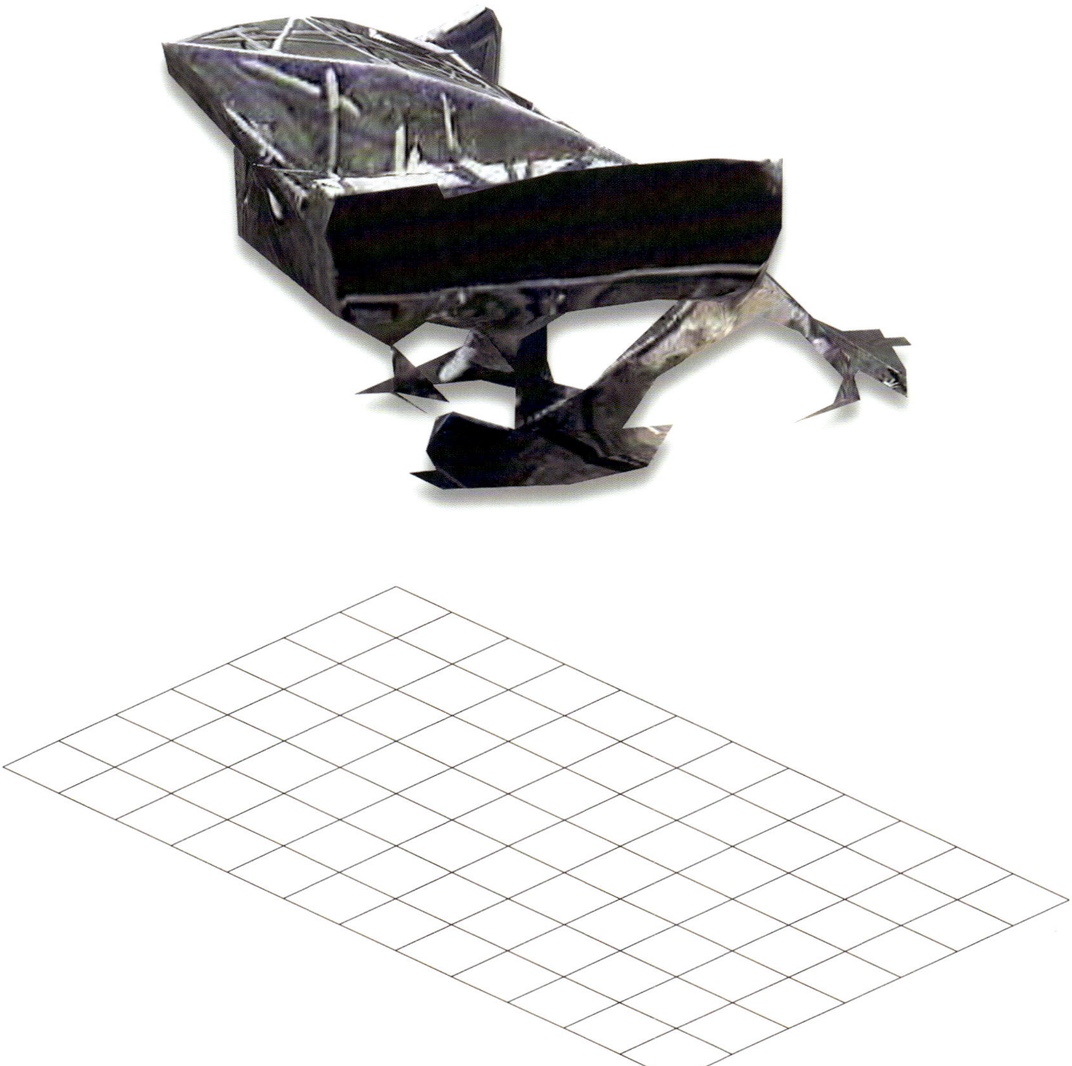

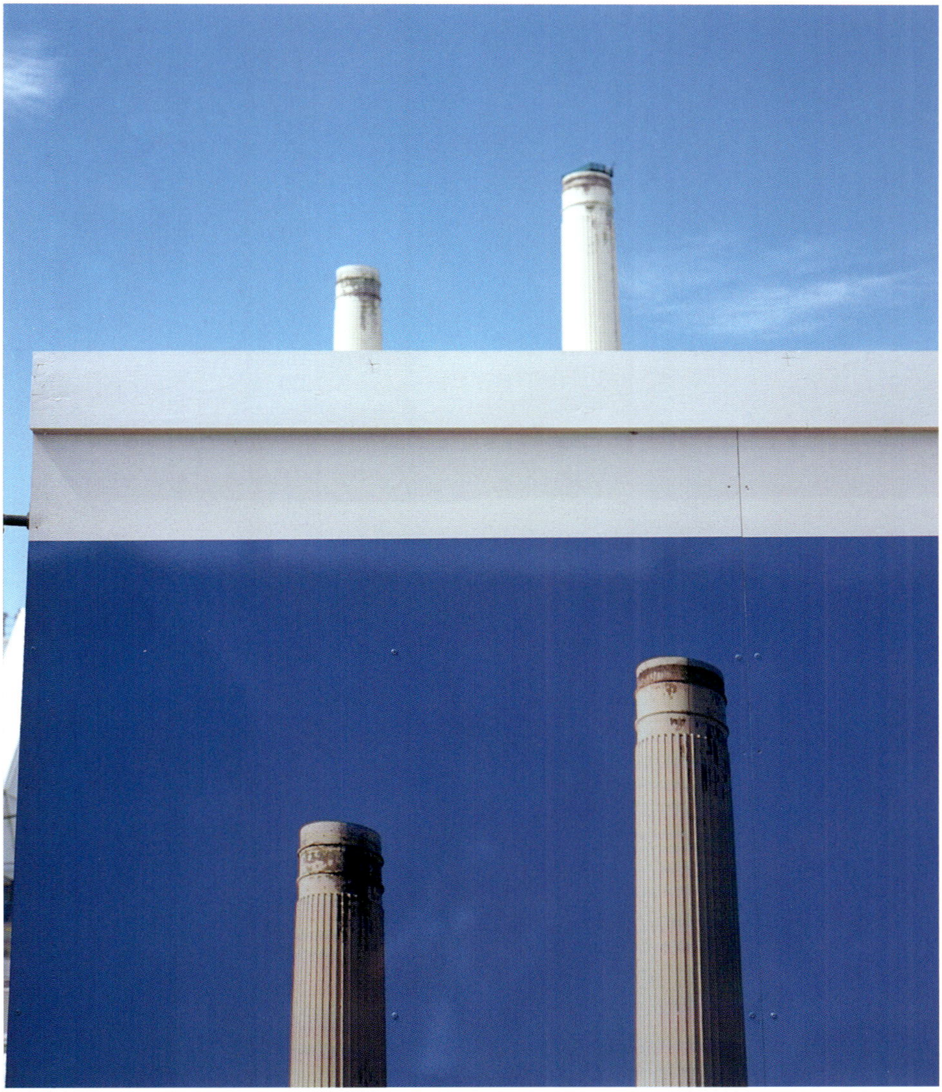

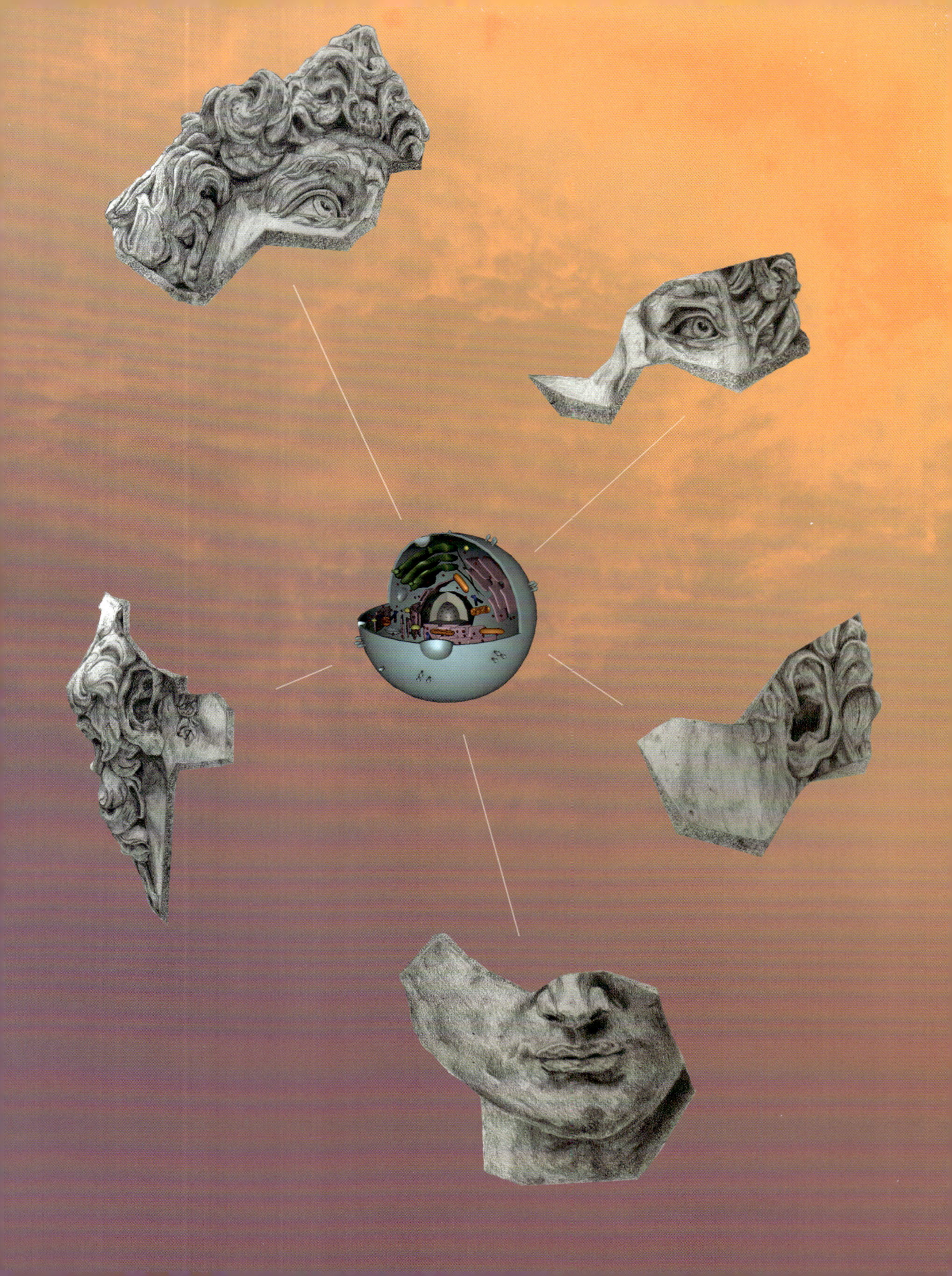

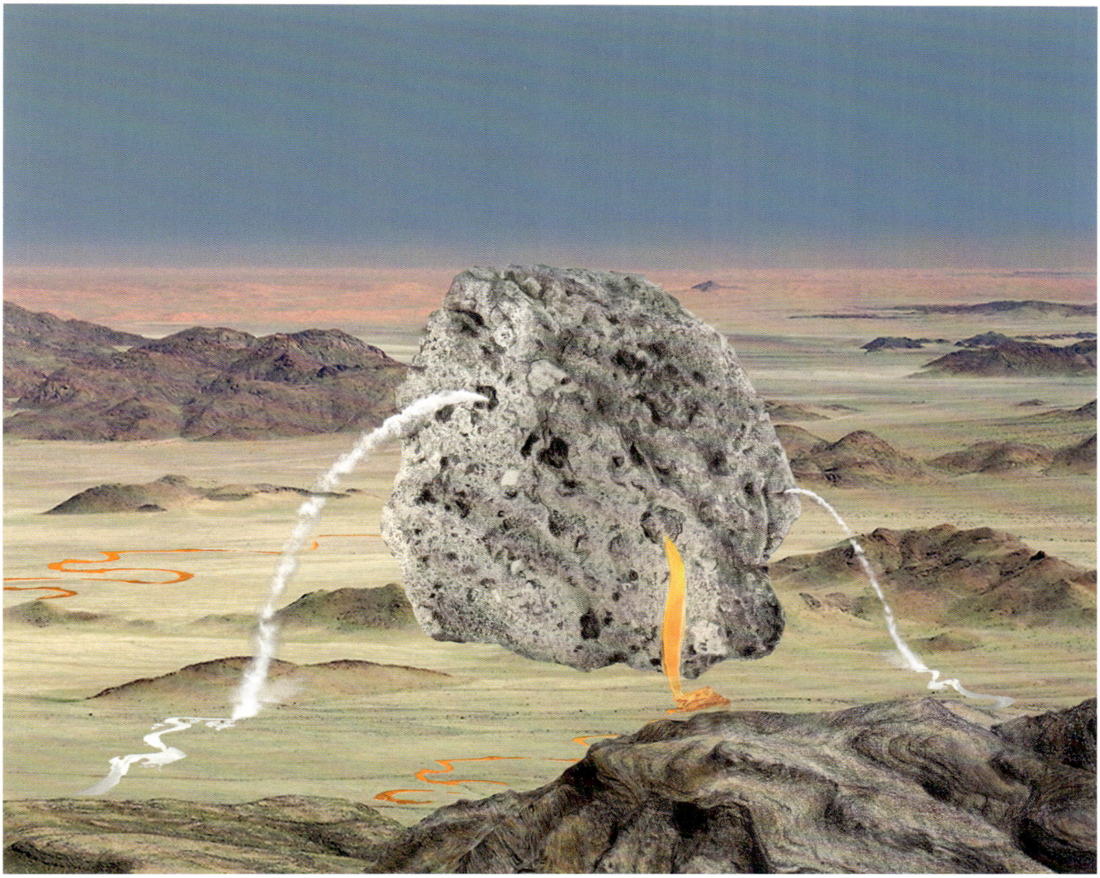

Shame on you.
Shame on you.

Shouted at visitors.

Approaching the entrance, a card in your pocket. This is your ticket and it says Community Leader.

Shame.

Blowing whistles, banging drums. Among their number, a three-piece band, a man with a GoPro on his forehead.

Smile, one shrieks.

flash

They stream video, tweet images of your arrival.

Security—*This way, keep moving.*

Crowd barriers separate them from you. Security is holding the crowd barriers up at either side of the entrance.

They wave placards, punch the air and jostle Security. There are smoke bombs.

Head down, walk fast. Don't look.

flash

You get in and the door is forced shut behind you. The light is hard and bright. A Venue Manager holding a chain. Confusion. She wraps it around the push bars, pulls it tight and clips shut a padlock.

There is a couple having an argument.

There is pounding at the door.
boom boom
Security is still out there.

Before we begin, says the Venue Manager, *can I get a bit of housekeeping out of the way?*

<u>Ritual sacrifice</u>
hand over your phone, take off your watch

<u>*Trapeze*</u>
the drinks sponsor, a rum-infused crème de cacao

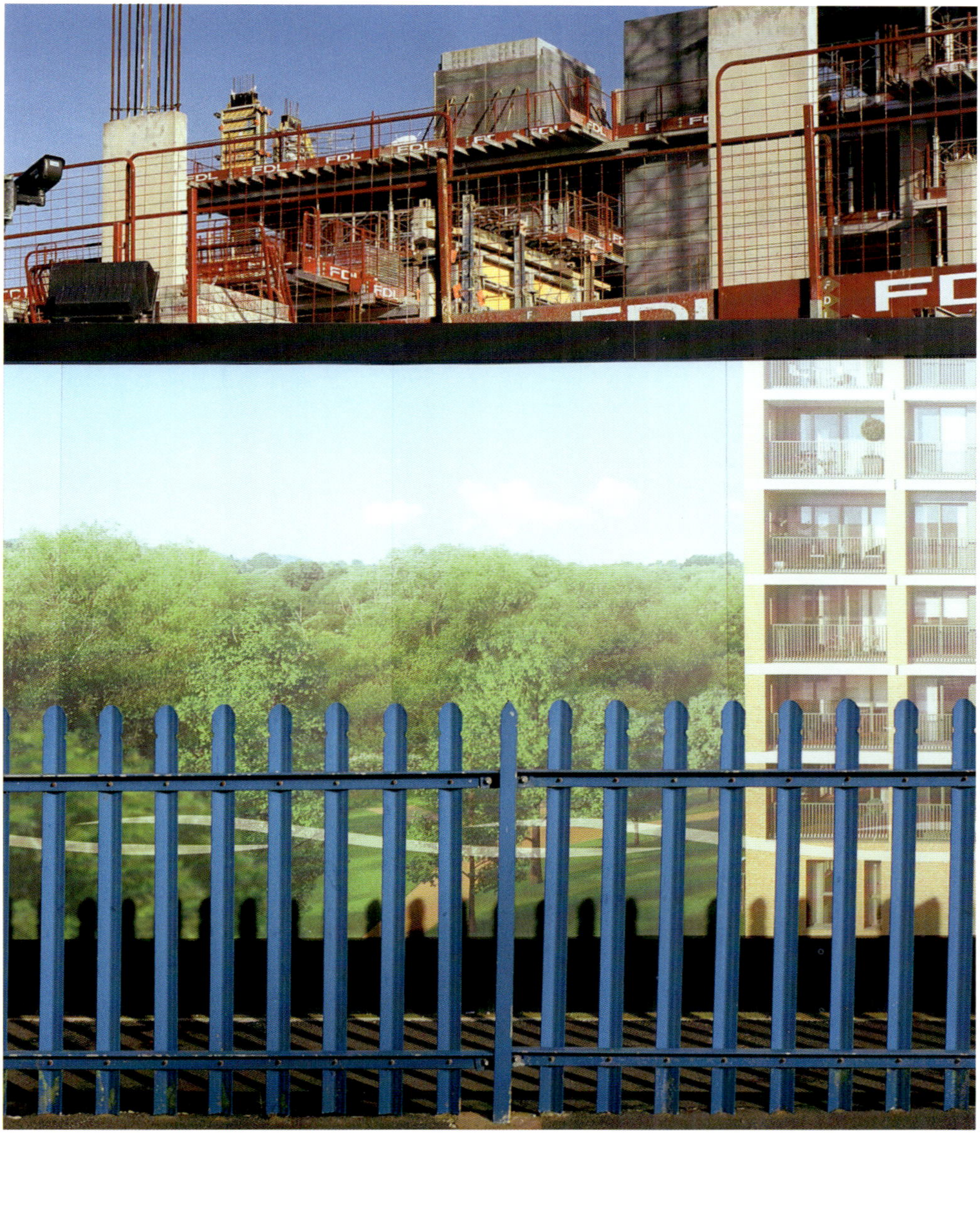
FDL

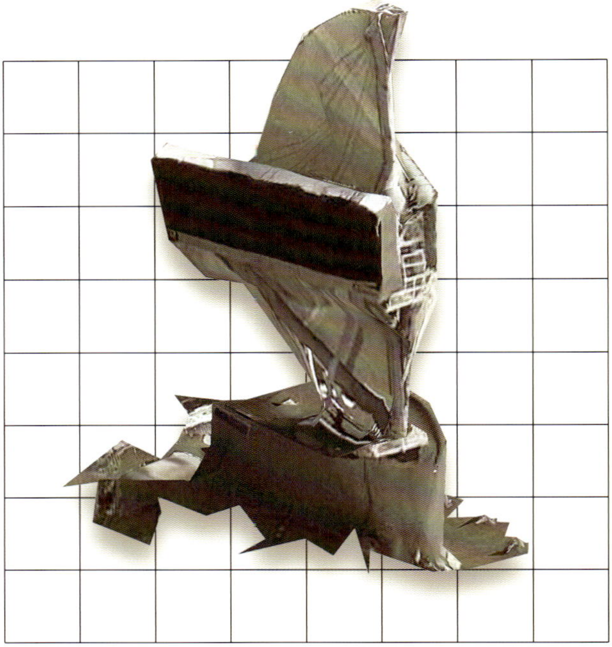

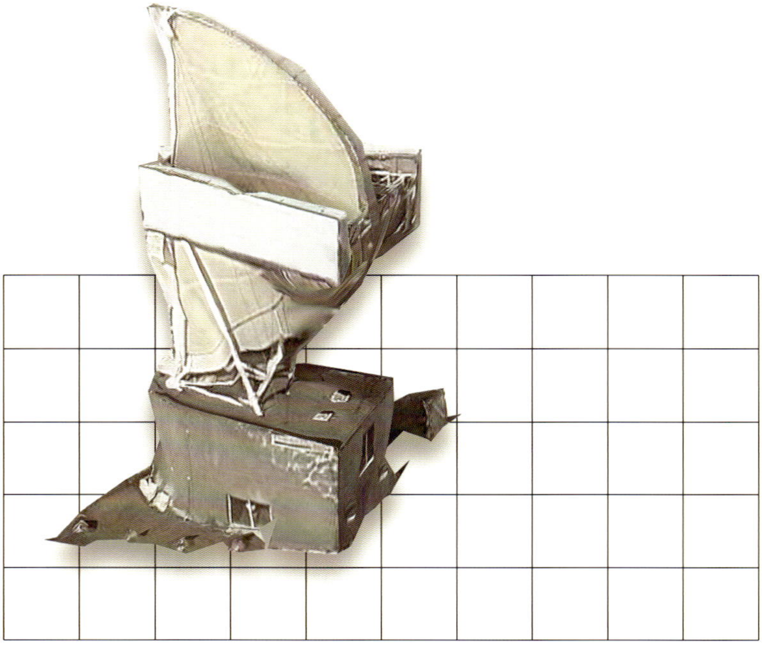

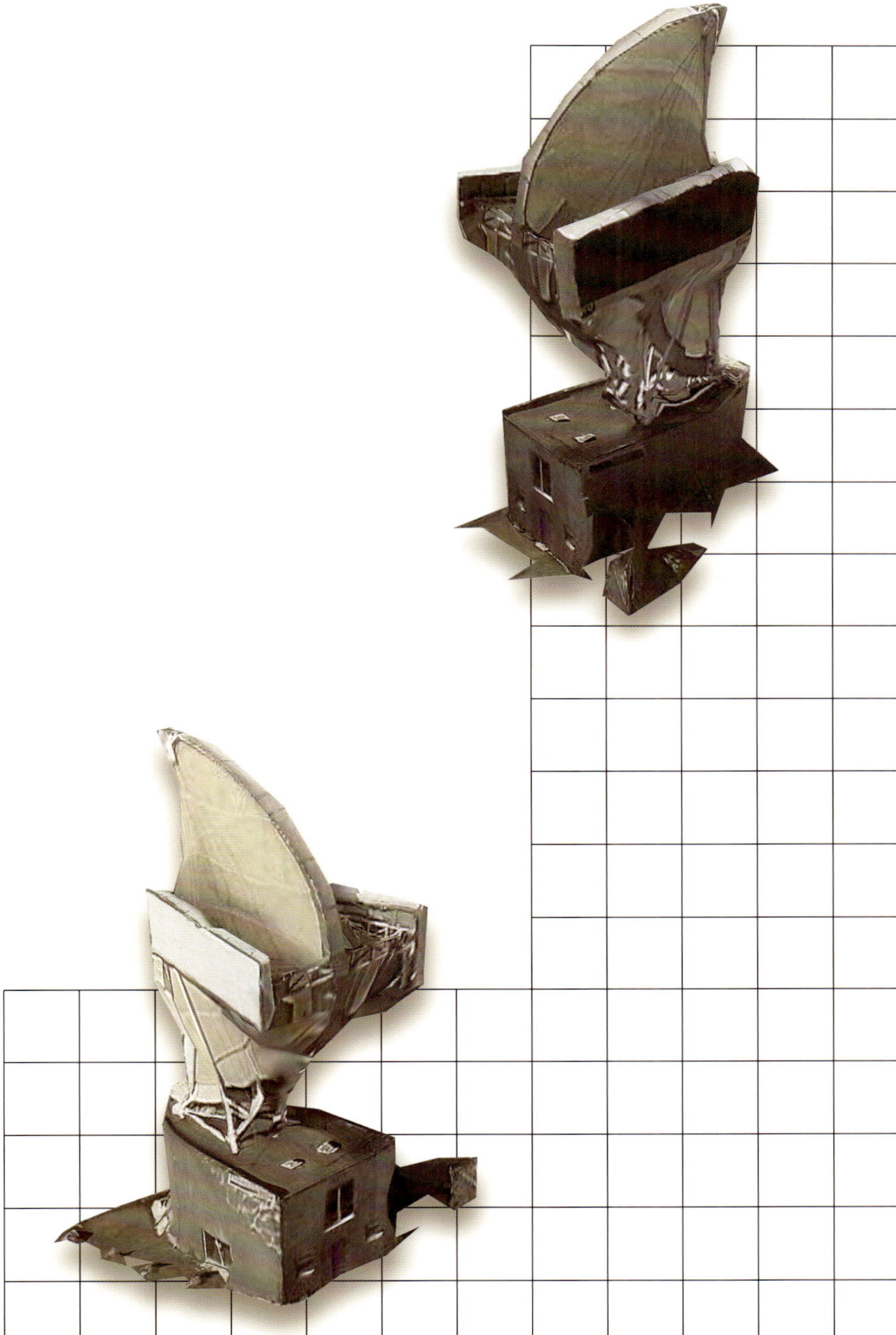

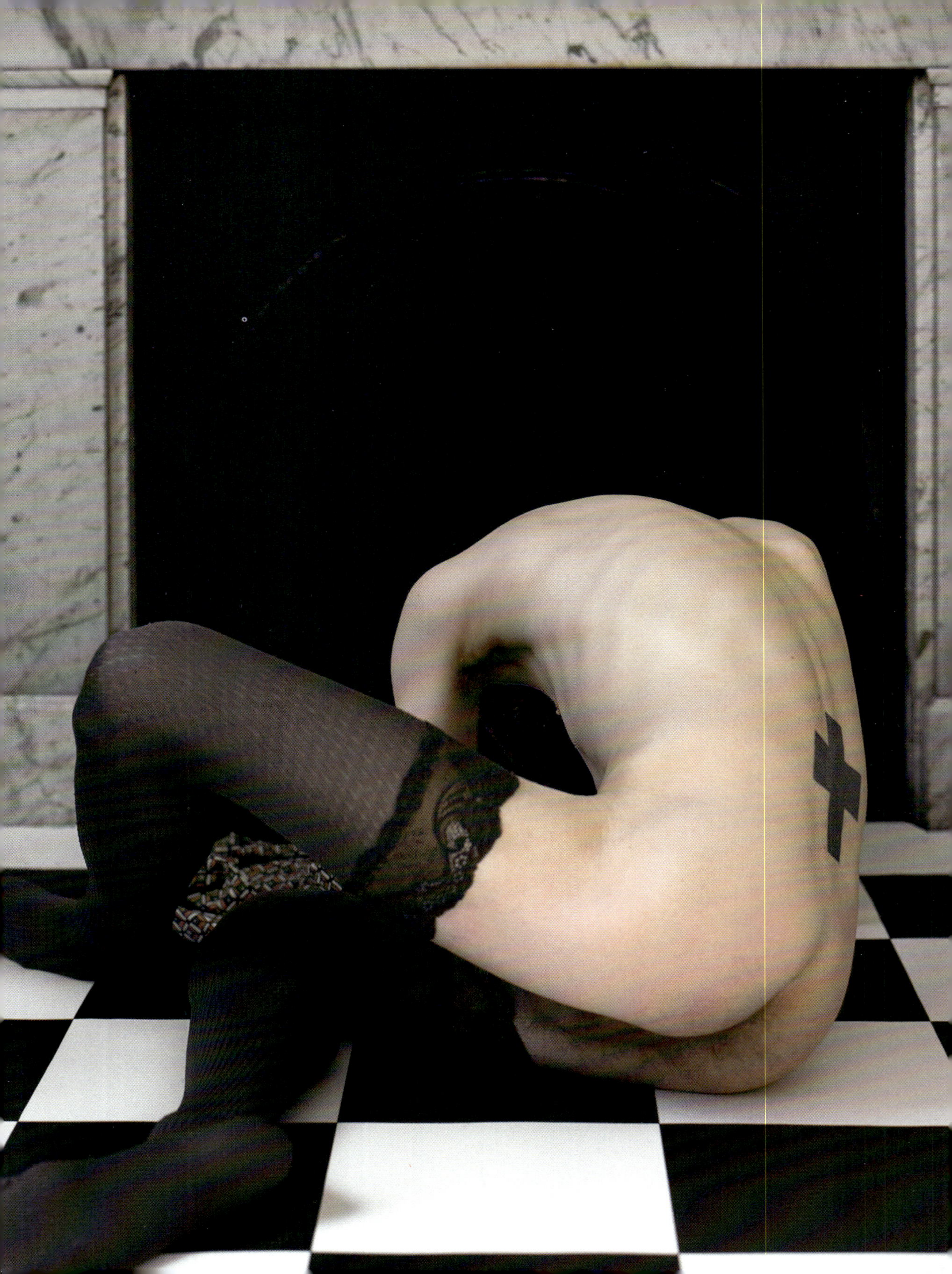

Trapeze

Well the whole um room was shrouded in this sort of green light am and the back wall was tiled So it was like white tiles but because of the light they were all tinged with green but like it was darker green at the top cos the light sort of faded as it went down the wall and in the middle of that wall there was this painting

but I guess it was more sort of like a sculptural painting because it was of mountains and sky

but where the mountains were it was er sort of like someone had balled up paper and newspaper and painted it so the mountains came out from the painting and then in front of that there was this architectural model of the campus

Well it wasn't of just the campus its was like the campus was on the like right hand side of the model and then there was the golf resort and then in front of that there was the whole city and that had this perspex top

and to the left of that there was this steel pole that had this like mesh on it like steel mesh and that like kind of separate isolated it all from the rest of the room

and then in front of the architectural model was these erm I guess they were sort of like palm trees but they were more spindly like the the trunks were really really em tiny n thin n and the leaves were really really long and the leaves were green and really pointy and there must have been about like eight or twelve in a cluster at the very top of the um trunk and that was set in this bark chipping
So the floor is terracotta tiles and the there was this um square hole that the palm trees were in that was filled with bark clippings and then in front of that
there was this um boat[1] well it was like made out of like wicker and straw

but I'm I'm not sure if its open to the public or is it just for people in the um who go to the university Because

I only went there to get catalogues because the the b' I went to the biennale and it was on at this disused dairy factory and the only am they hadn't they had run out of catalogues

and when I arrived there was this woman outside the building and she was sat at this table and she had am a magazine in front of her and then she had a bottle of water well it was like she had orange squash but it was in er like an old am like Evian bottle and then she had an am umbrella and it was raining but she didn't have the umbrella up am and she kept apologising to me about the rain and saying that she w' oh she didn't want me to get wet am but then she said that she couldn't give me her umbrella because it was the only one she had And I was like I don't I don't expect to have the umbrella I just I just want a catalogue and she was wearing this like black polo-neck and this really large crystal and diamanté necklace

So I went round the exhibition and when I came out she said that there was two catalogues in the university and then she gave me directions of how to get there

and she said that when I arrived to the university I'd see this kinetic sculpture and to go into the red-brick building So when we go there we saw the kinetic sculpture and it was in this um square pool of water and then around that there was four smaller squares and the kinetic sculpture was in was rotating in the largest one

but there was four red-brick buildings that like spanned all in front of the um kinetic sculpture so we just went into the first one on the right and that's when we am when we s when we saw the um painting

and I I don't know why it's in there

and um

like who who made it

and how it ended up in a basement

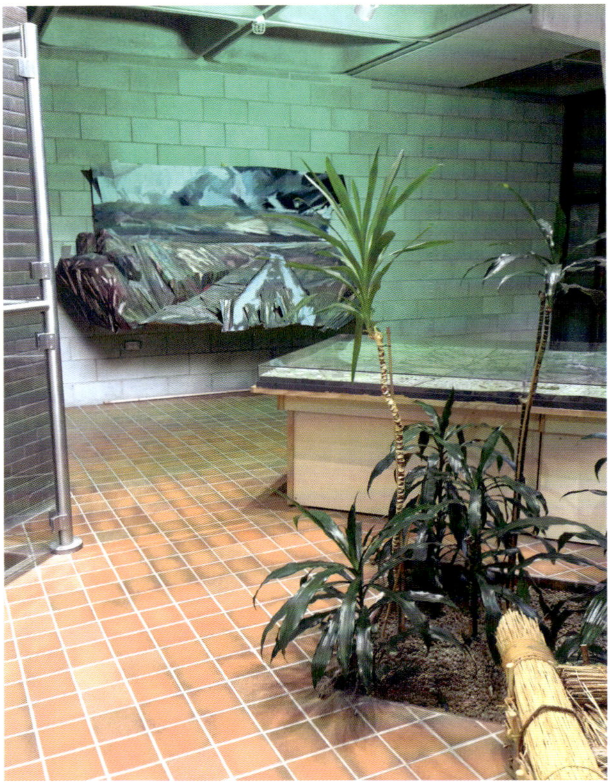

1

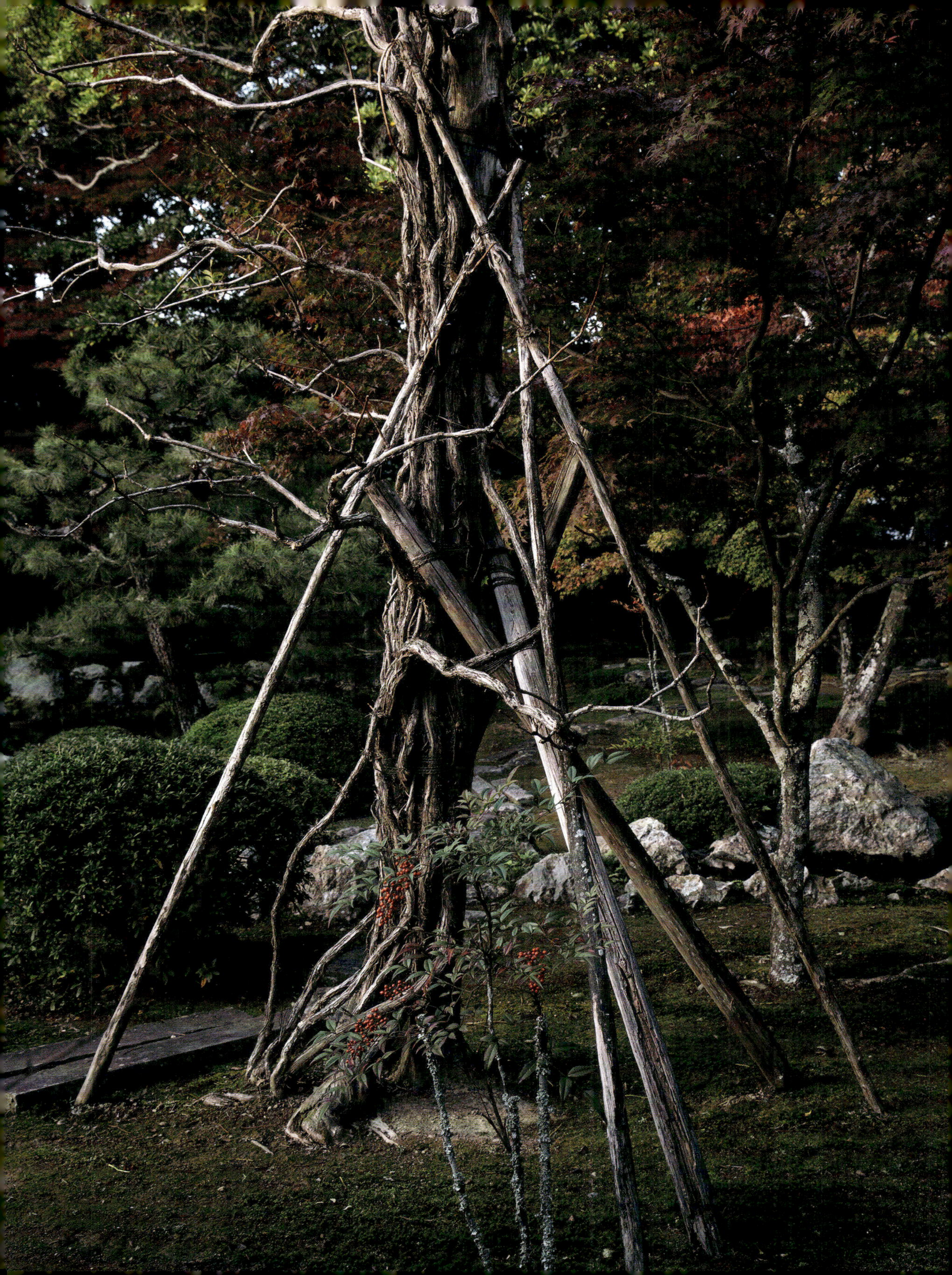

Exit

sign

Platters of *Trapeze*–based cocktails are offered with a question—*Live dangerously?*

<u>Exit sign</u>
a man running, an arrow, an open door

But that exit is chained shut.

<u>A man hiding</u>
cap and sunglasses, beard and headphones

tick tick tick tick from his headphones.

There is also an old classmate —avoid—now is not the time. Waiters suspenseful, bear colourful cocktails—*Live dangerously?*

Calm gathers. There is mingling, you meet people. Consultants, Analysts, Executives, Fundraisers. Leaders in their fields.

A man's voice, approaching from behind—*I'll be your Guru.*

You turn and share a look.

Show me your card, he says.

Community Leader, he reads. *Those protests came from Community Leaders.*

He takes you from the crowd.

Conversation coming like—
Do you consider yourself an extrovert?
Would you prefer to be a private person?
What are your traditional goals?

This is taking place in a corridor when—quick, hide—a former teacher passes. Recognising an opportunity, your Guru presses a false moustache under your nose.

Though it looks ridiculous, it is a cloak of invisibility.

Governed only by pleasure, could you be like that man in cap and sunglasses? Could it be he does not wish to be recognised? His T-shirt has written on it GHOST STORIES.

Another exit sign.

Its green light throbs. Feelings of disconnection. There is no air in this place. It is bright, windowless and hot.

Have you looked into yourself lately?

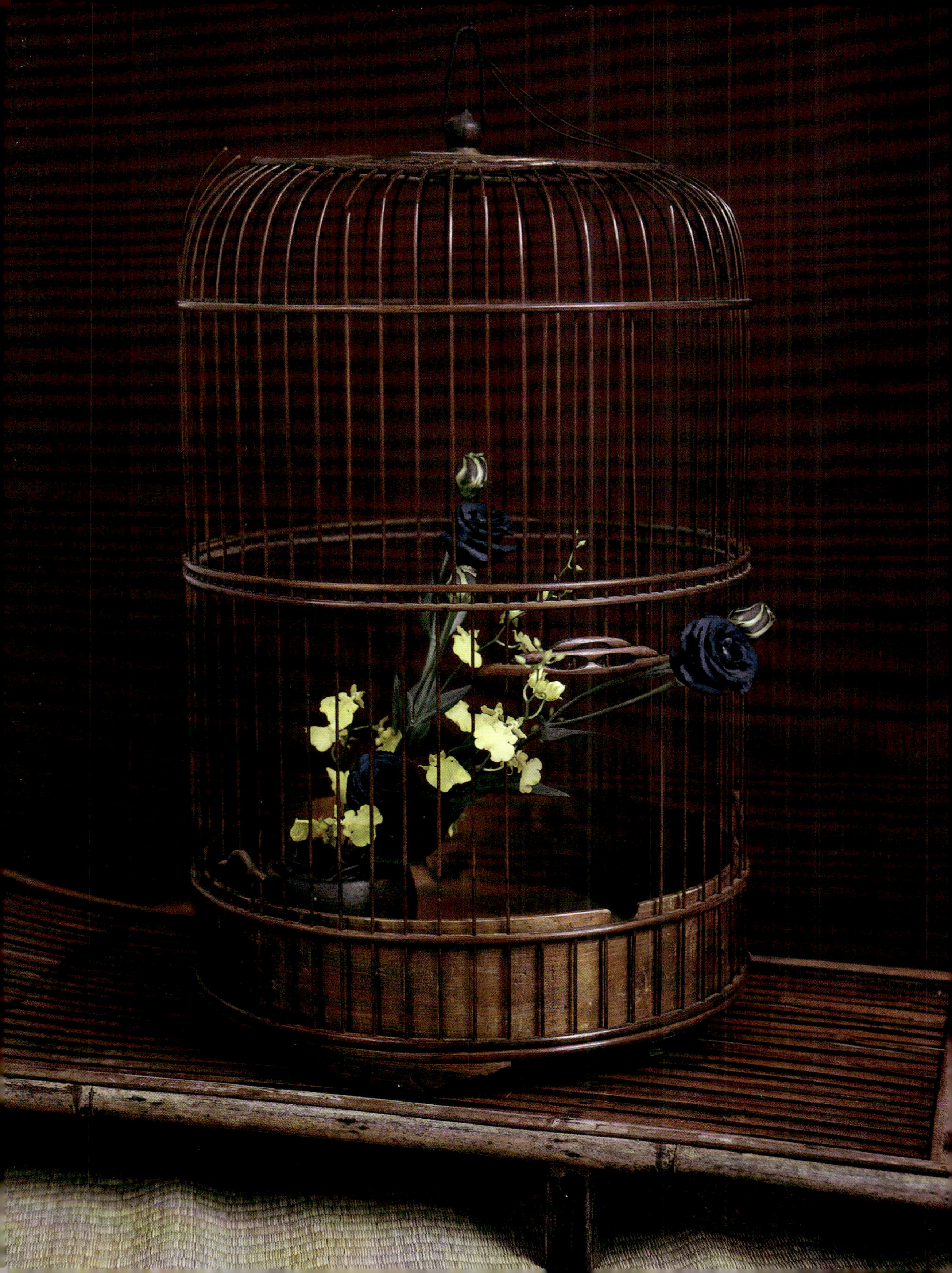

Persons in Location

Husband: aged forty-four, white, unemployed. (DD)
Wife: aged thirty to thirty-nine, white, divorcee, employed. (DID)
Kid: aged seven to twelve; white. (OCD)

Mother: aged thirty-four, black, unmarried, employed. (SZO)
Teenager: aged fifteen; mixed race; single. (AD)

Bishop, California: a small city where Westerns are filmed.

Follow the road four point seven miles to the interstate; then another two point five to Bishop. Traveling is done on foot, unless a local offers a hitch. This location is a part of the government-owned Owens Valley that operates as a water supply for Los Angeles. The Teenager is the son from the Husband's previous relationship; The Kid is his half brother.
The characters come from and are limited to quantifiable fact. The space hasn't been altered. "Since none of the characters or incidents of this volume are fictitious, the names of most persons, and nearly all names of places, are altered.
The ages given, and tenses throughout, save where it is otherwise obvious or deliberately ambiguous, are as of the summer of 1936."

J. Agee & W. Evans, Let Us Now Praise Famous Men (1941), p.16.

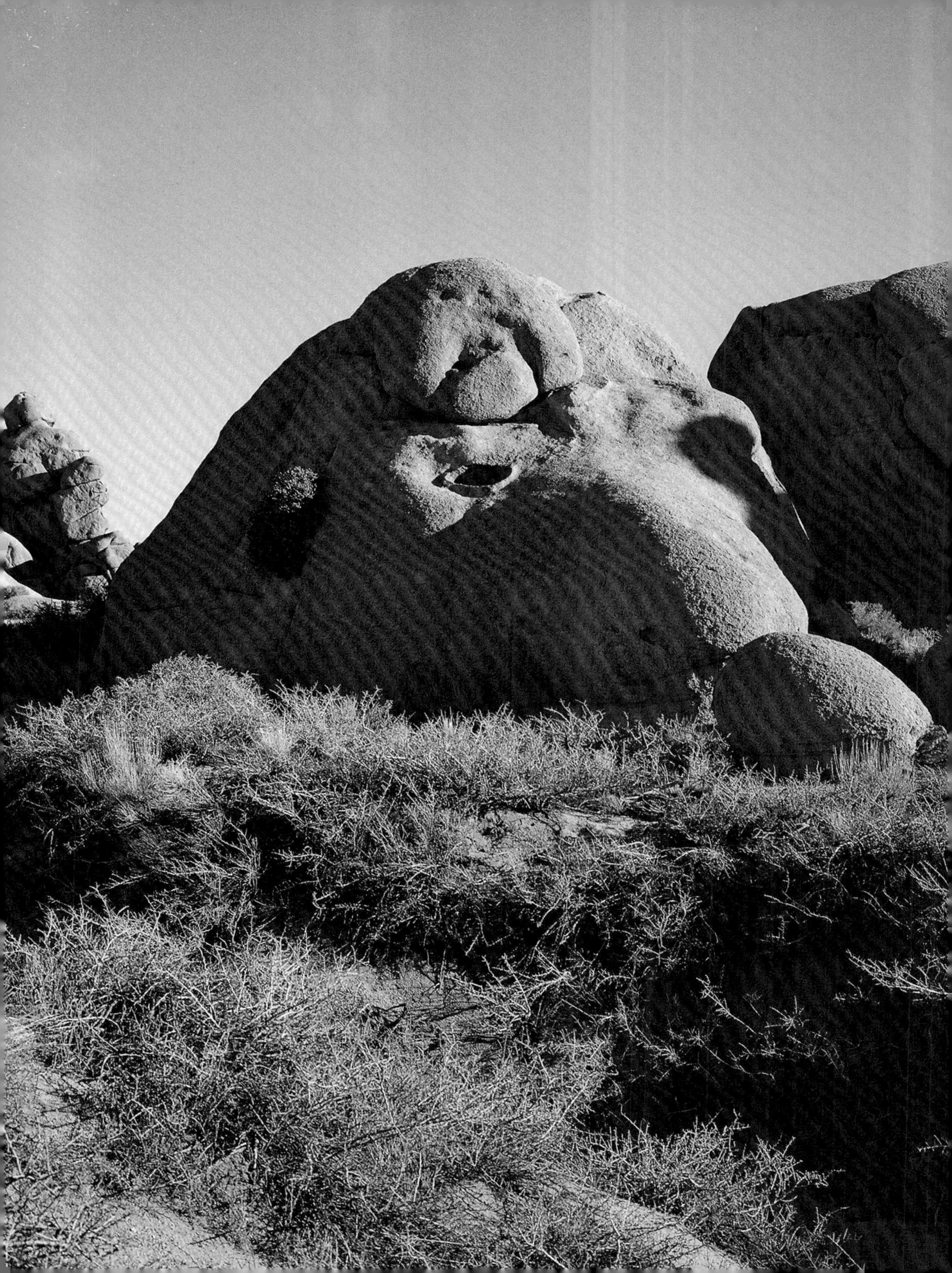

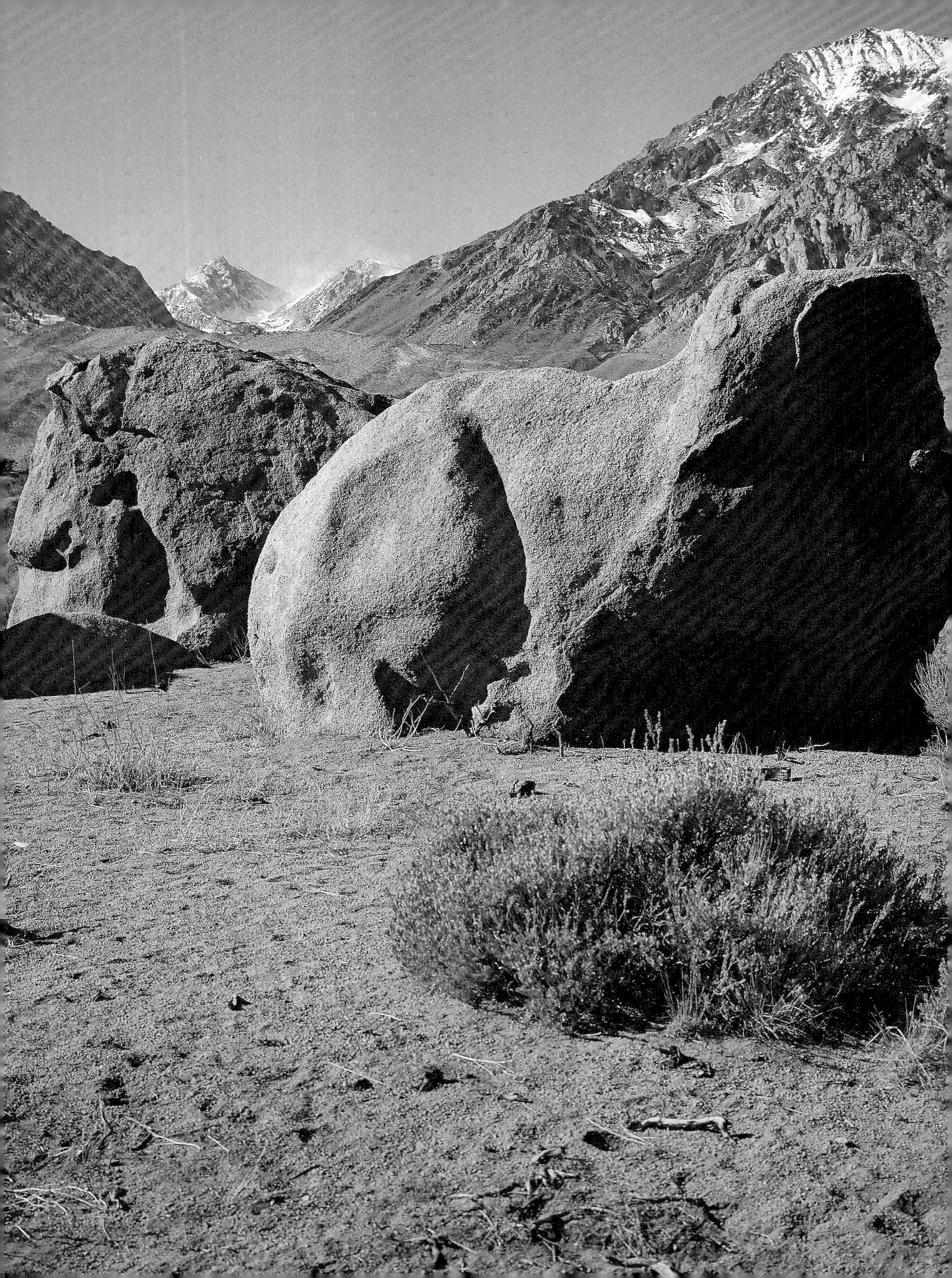

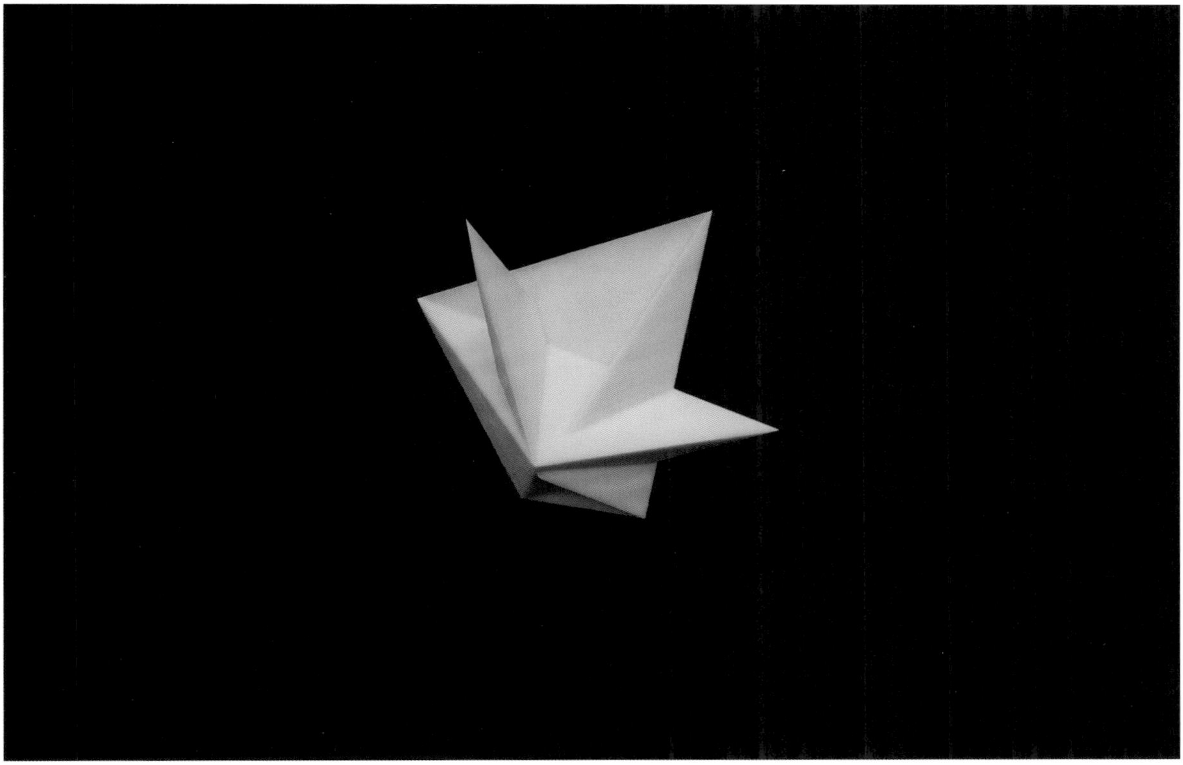

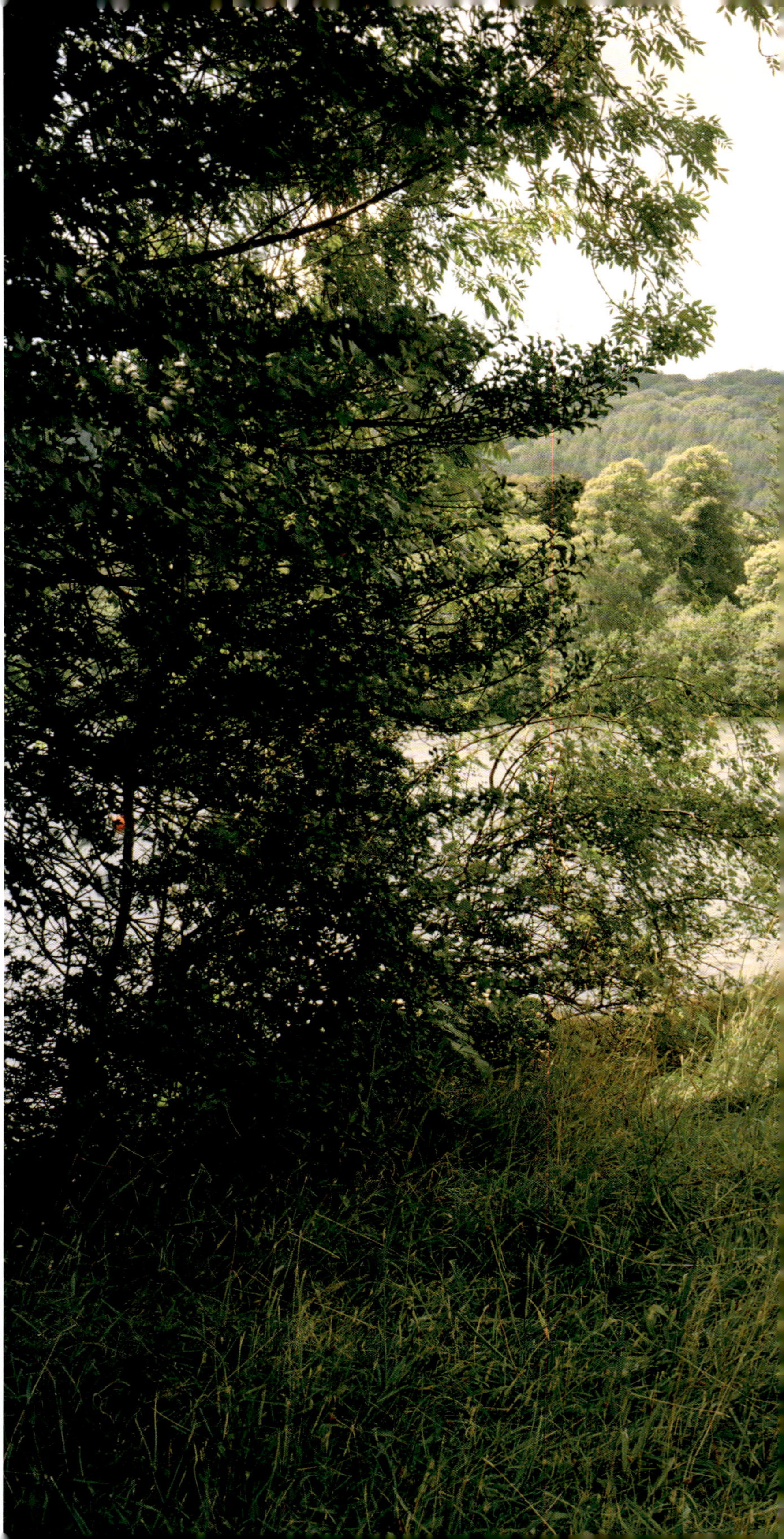

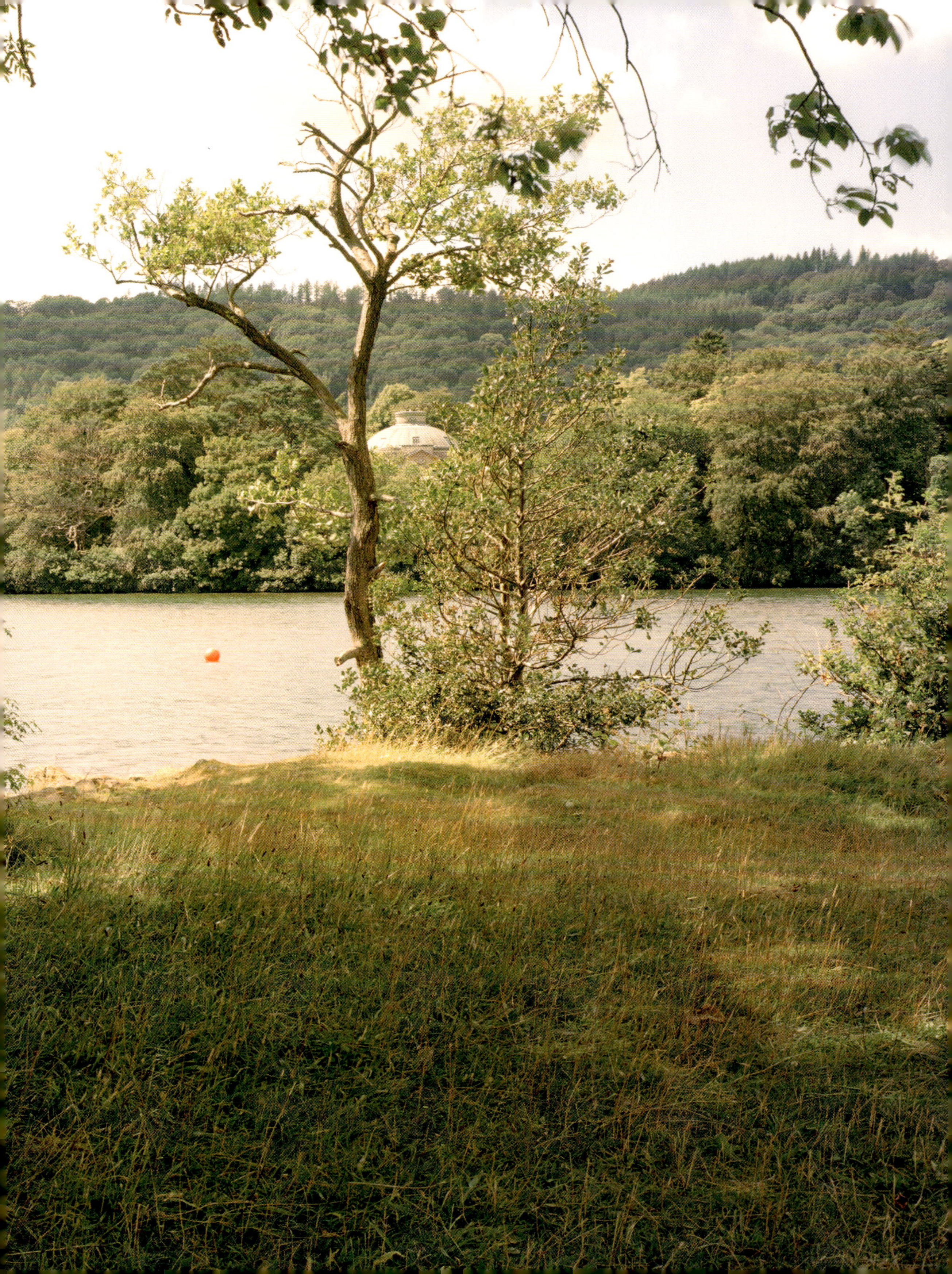

1 In the beginning God created the heaven and the earth.

00110001001000000010010010110111000100000011101000110100001100101001000
00011000100110010101100111011010010110111001101110011010010110111001100110
0111001000000100011101101111011001000010000001100011011100100110010101
1000010111010001100101011001000010000000111010001101000011001010010000 0
0110100001100101011000010111011001100101011011100010000001100001011011
1001100100001000000111010001101000011001010010000000110010101100001 0111
00100111010001101000000101110

3 And God said, Let there be light: and there was light.

0011001100100000010000010110111001100100001000000100011101101111011001
000010000000111001101100001011010010110010000101100001000000100110001 10
0101011101000010000000111010001101000011001010111001001100101001000000 1
1000100110010100100000011011000110100101100111011010000111010000111010
00100000001100001011011100110010000100000001110100011010000110010101 1100
10011001010010000000111011101100001011100110010000000110110001101001011 0
01110110100001110100000101110

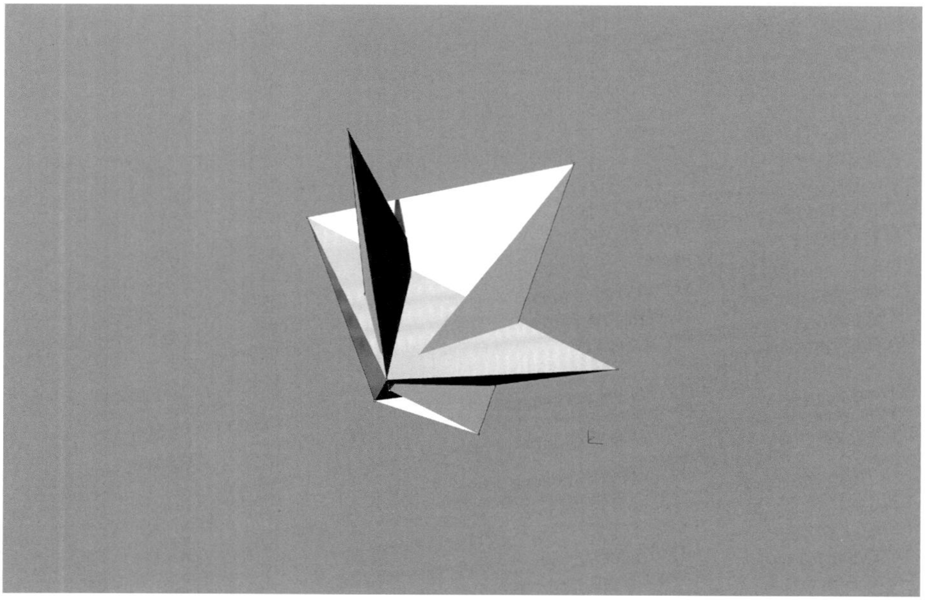

A man

hiding

143
SECOND
STREET

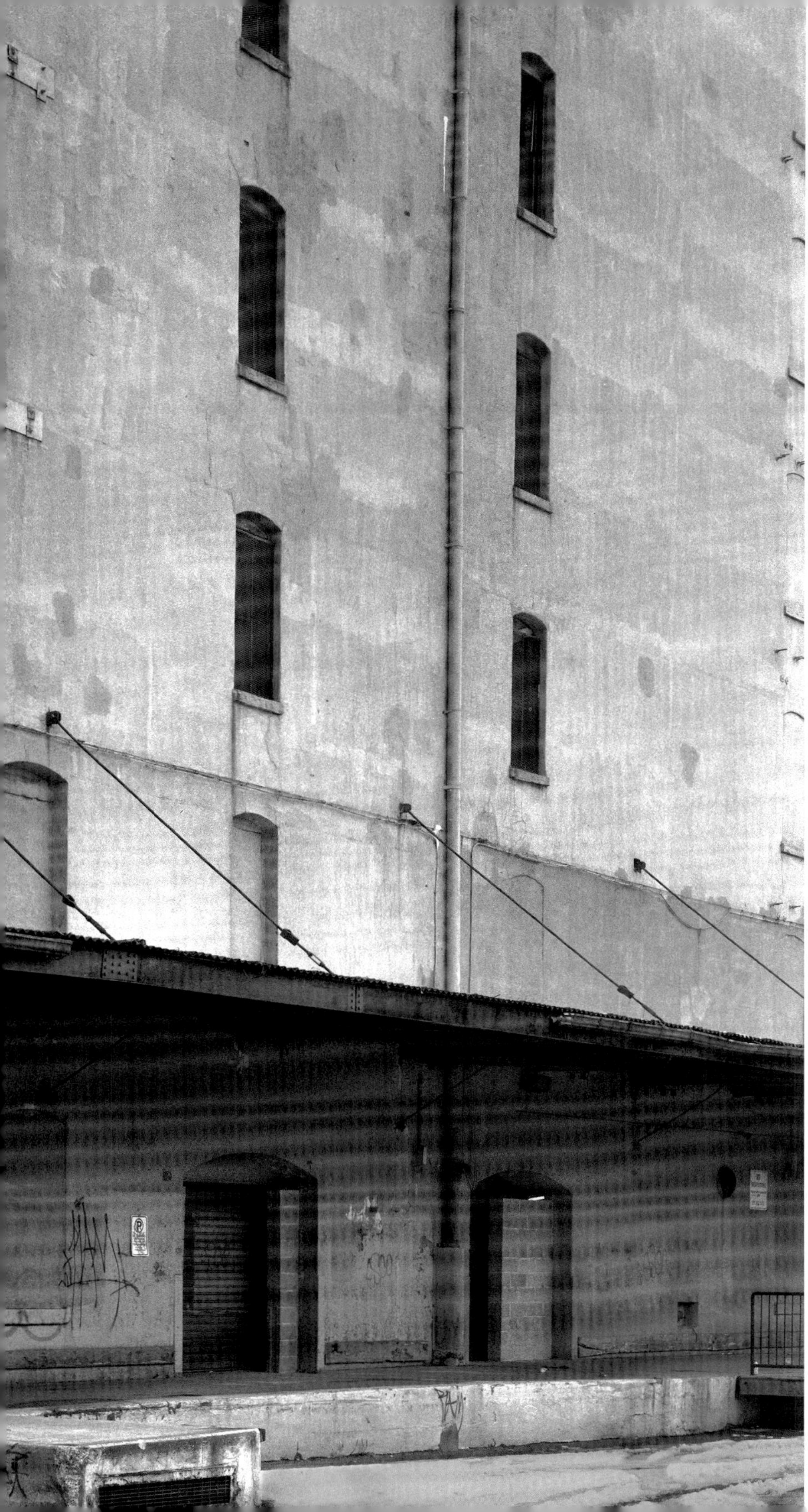

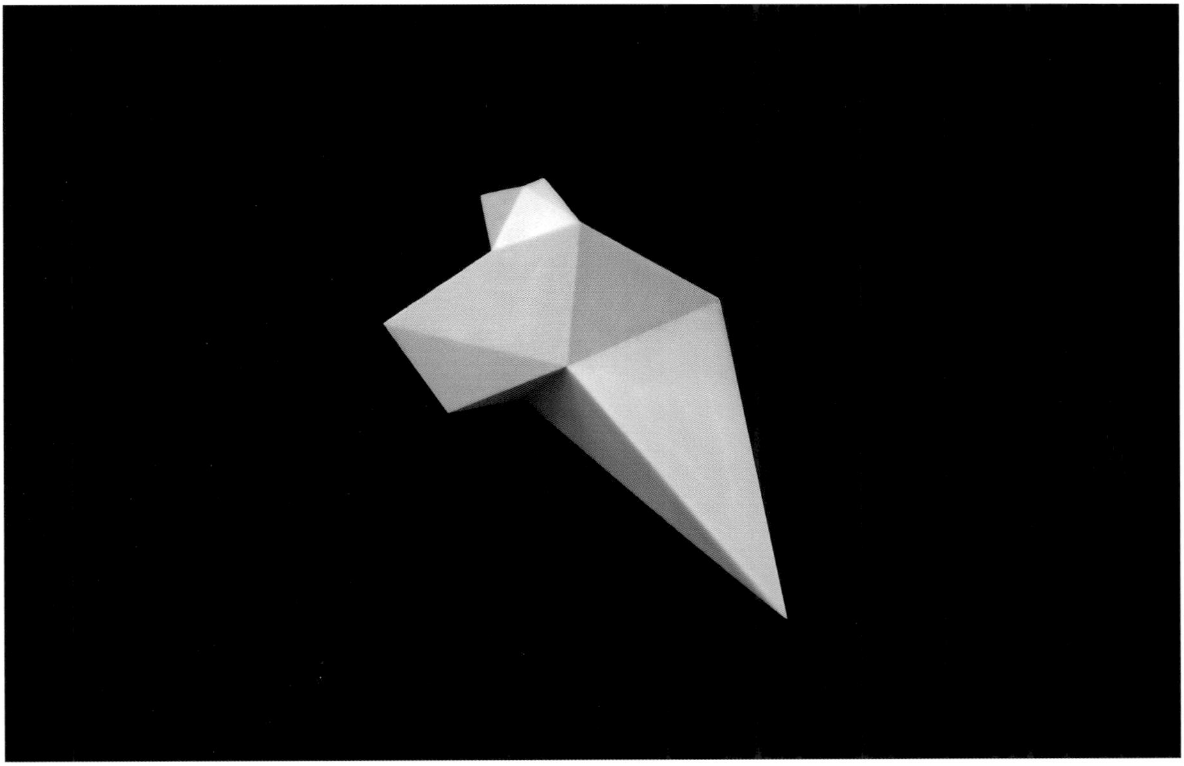

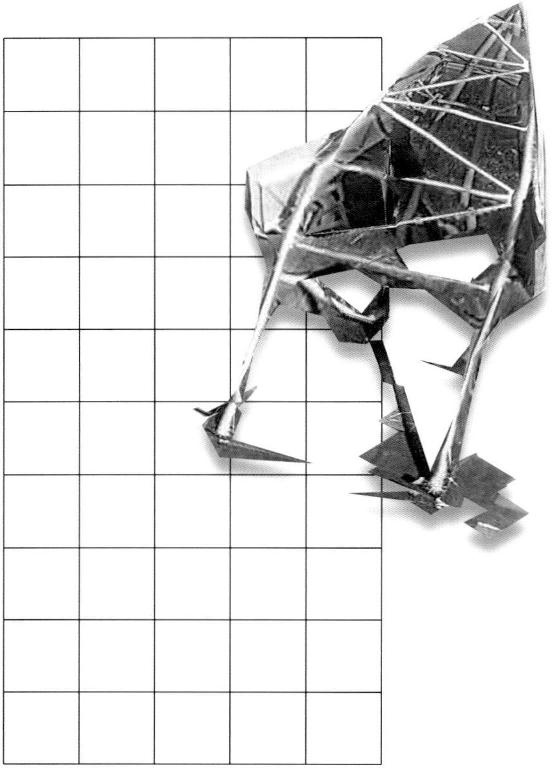

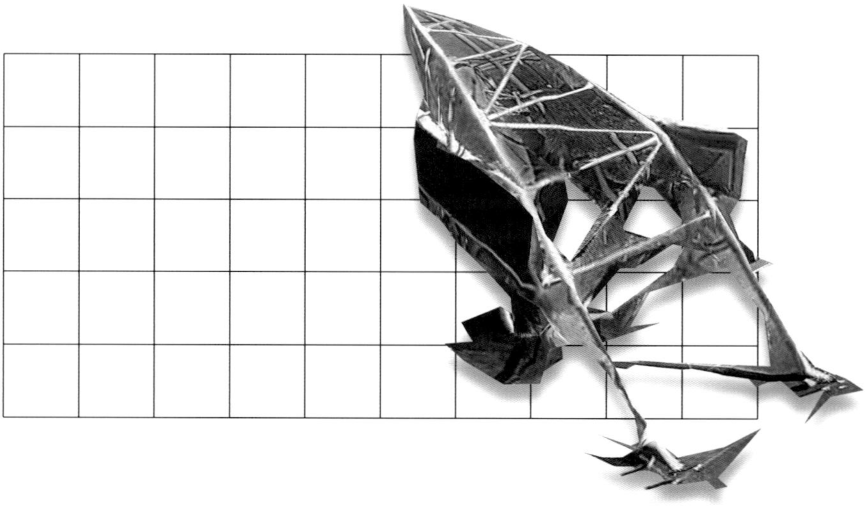

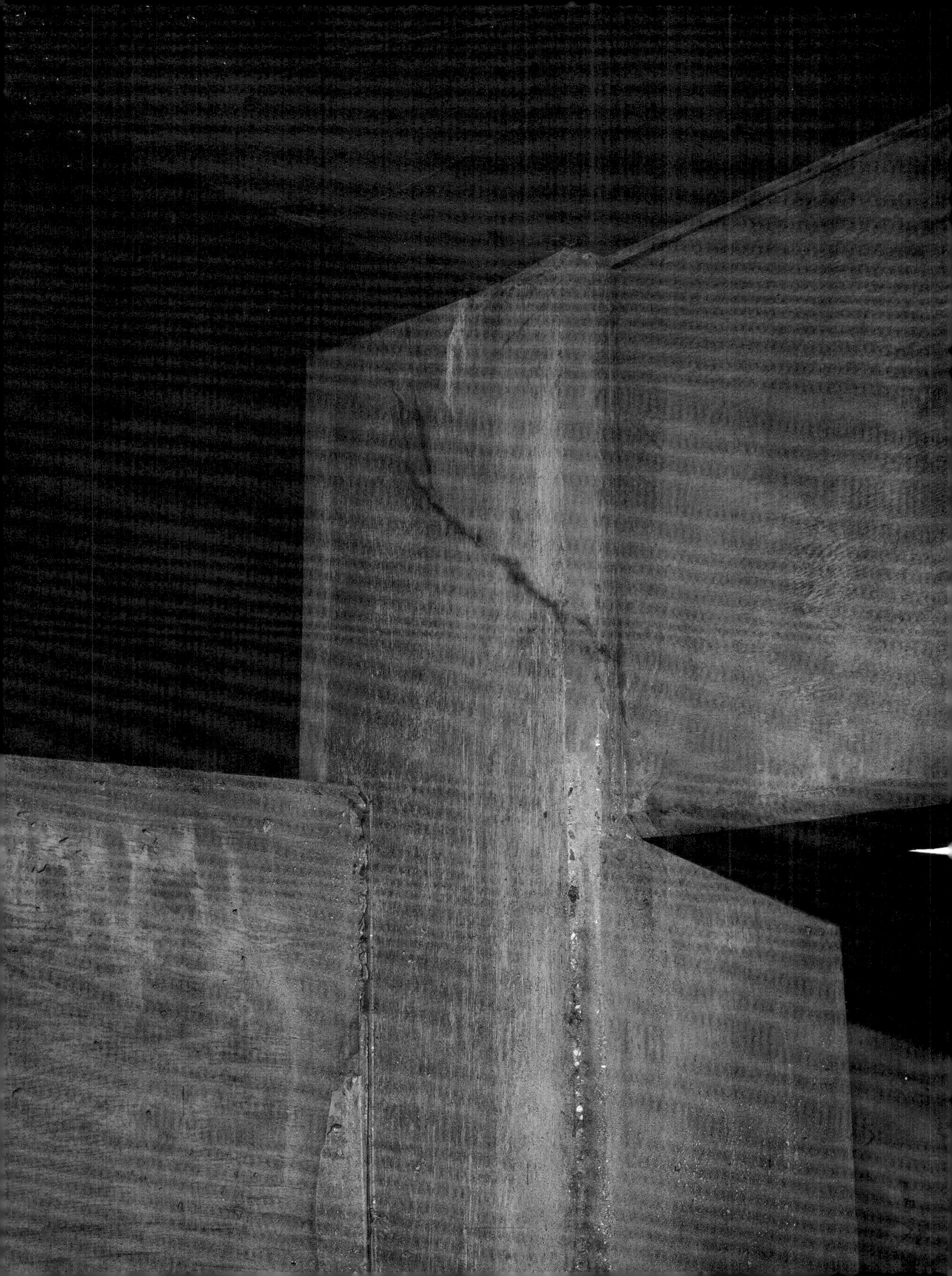

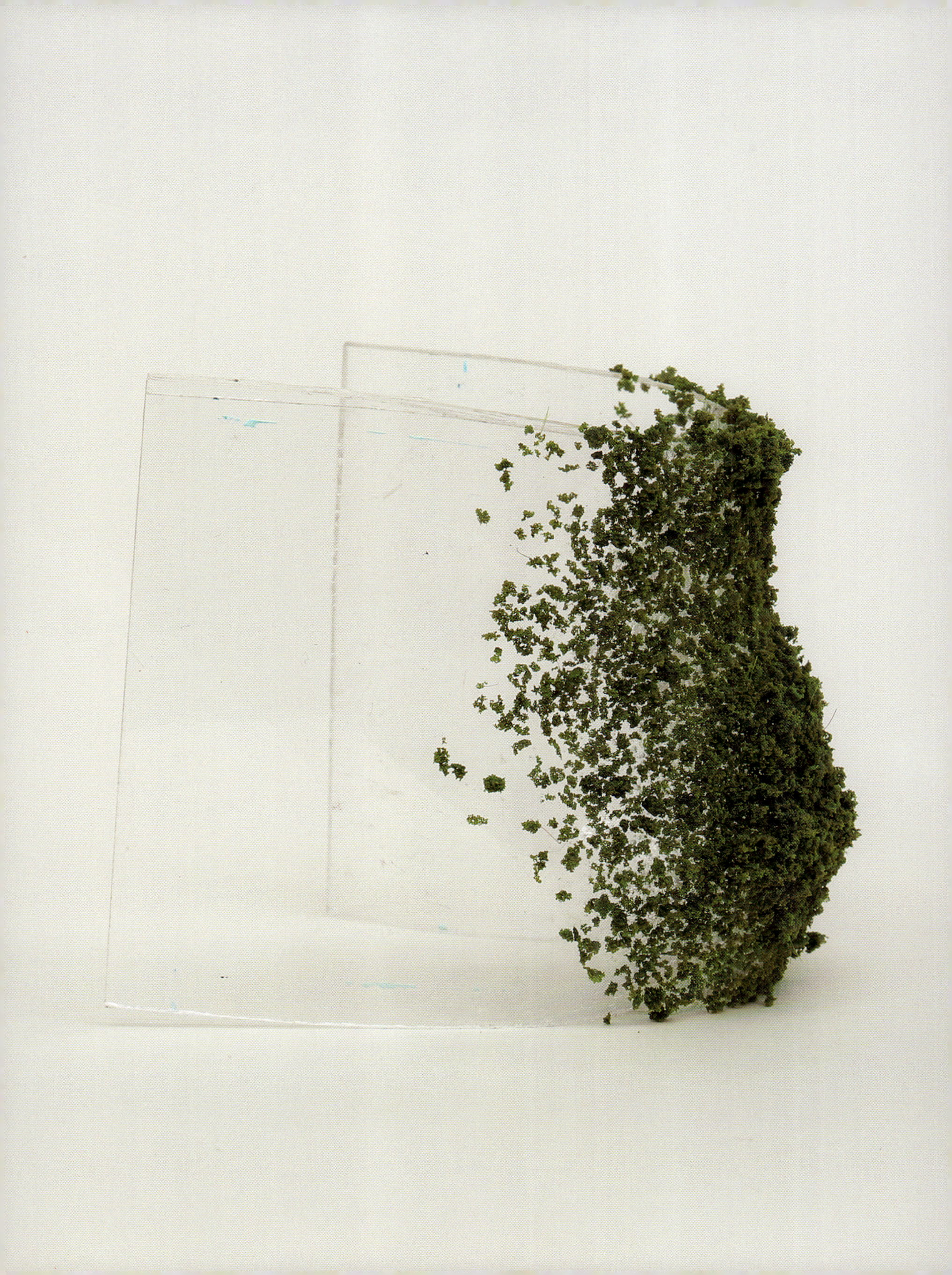

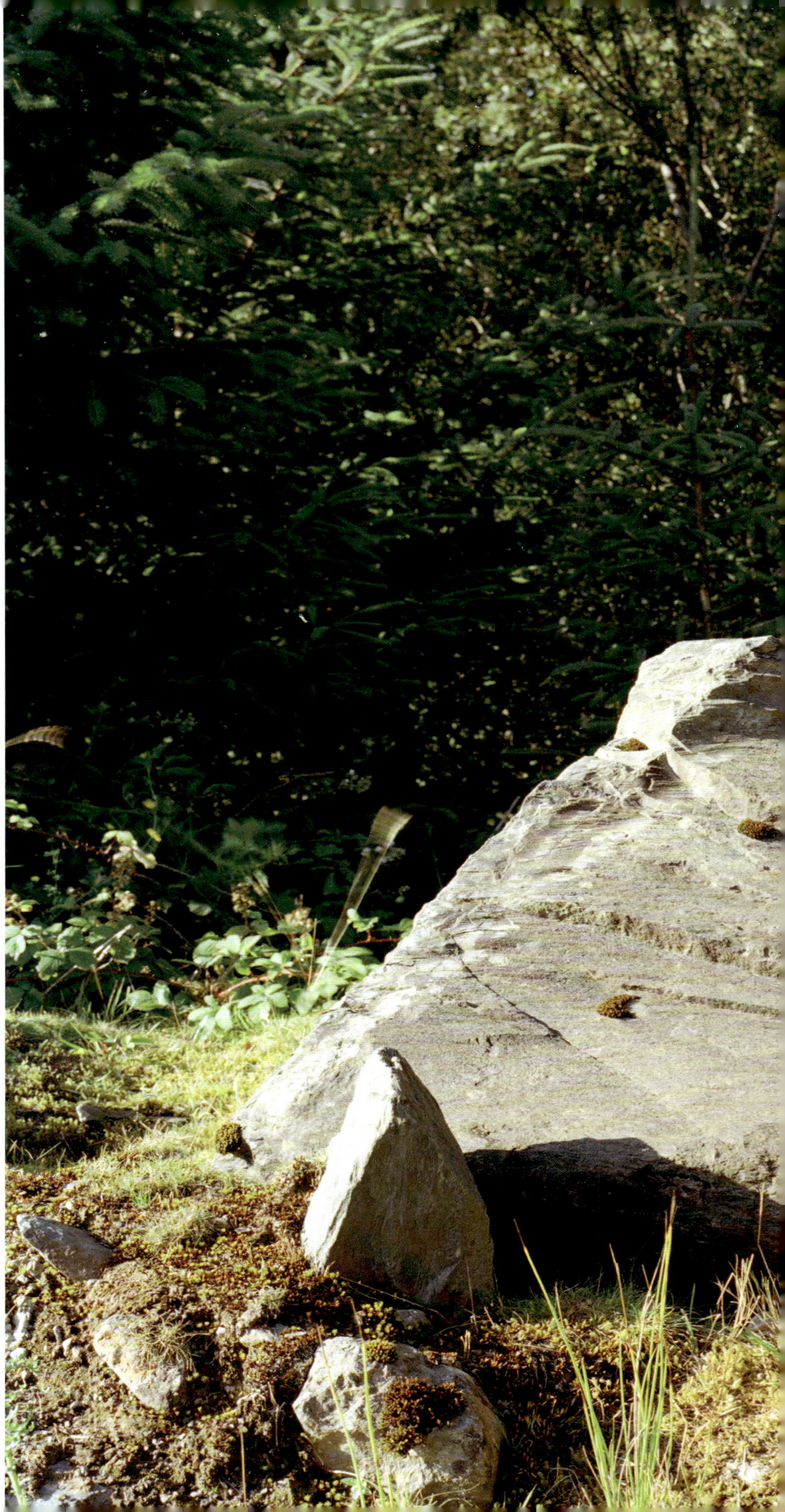

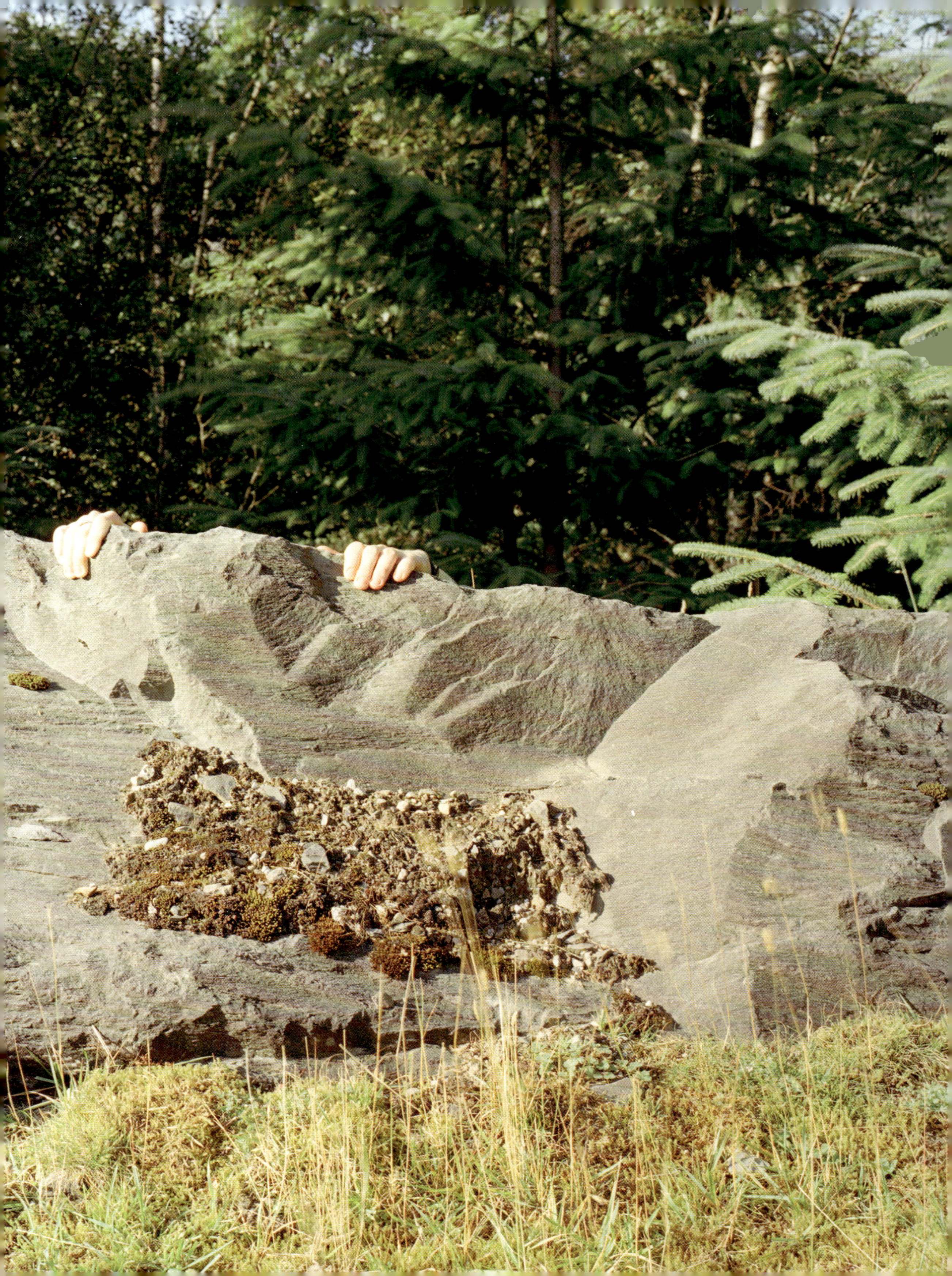

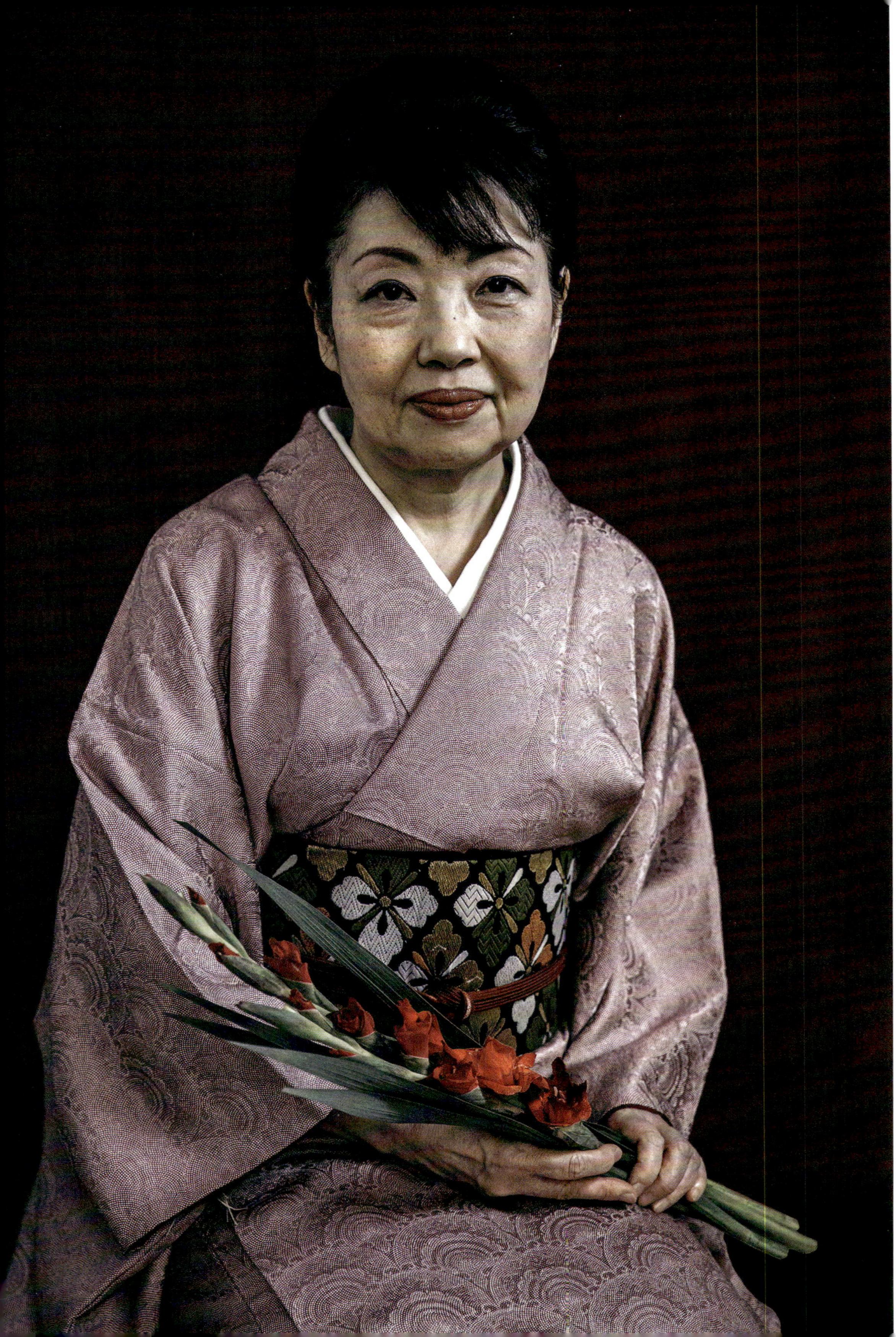

Watching your Guru,
wondering how far to take this—
We've met before.
That was a long, long time ago.
Should we talk about it?
Picking up an artist CV, he
reads—*Born in 1991, lives and*
works in London, what else is
there?
Live dangerously? a waiter
asks.

will know this figure. Who stands
before me is obliterated. Hashtag
Shame will be your new name.
The right to be forgotten? You can
only wish. In their portrait, you are
bleached, disingenuous. A drained
face of hatred. Is that something
to show the grandchildren?

<u>The grandchildren</u>
picturing green-skin flesh-eating
pink-eye zombies

<u>I am discovering new stations</u>
<u>in life</u>

Walk to me, walk to me, says a
woman walking backwards.
She is taking pictures.
You follow, imagining she is an
Official Photographer.
Your Guru, head tilted,
inscrutable smile—*This isn't the*
first time your photo has been
taken today.

You can't go back. Out there,
your image shared, email
hacked, every detail of the
mundane, dispersed and etched
permanently. No friend, new lover

Waiting for a sign.
Dragged past a man whose arm
has tattooed GHOST STORIES in a
swirling scroll. A tell-tale moment
that calls—

I'm leaving, said the wind

it doesn't take much to bring you
back
sober and reasoned
collect those stated facts
deliver something
meaningful and plainspoken

who will break the Debt
Machine?

I am
discovering
new
stations
in
life

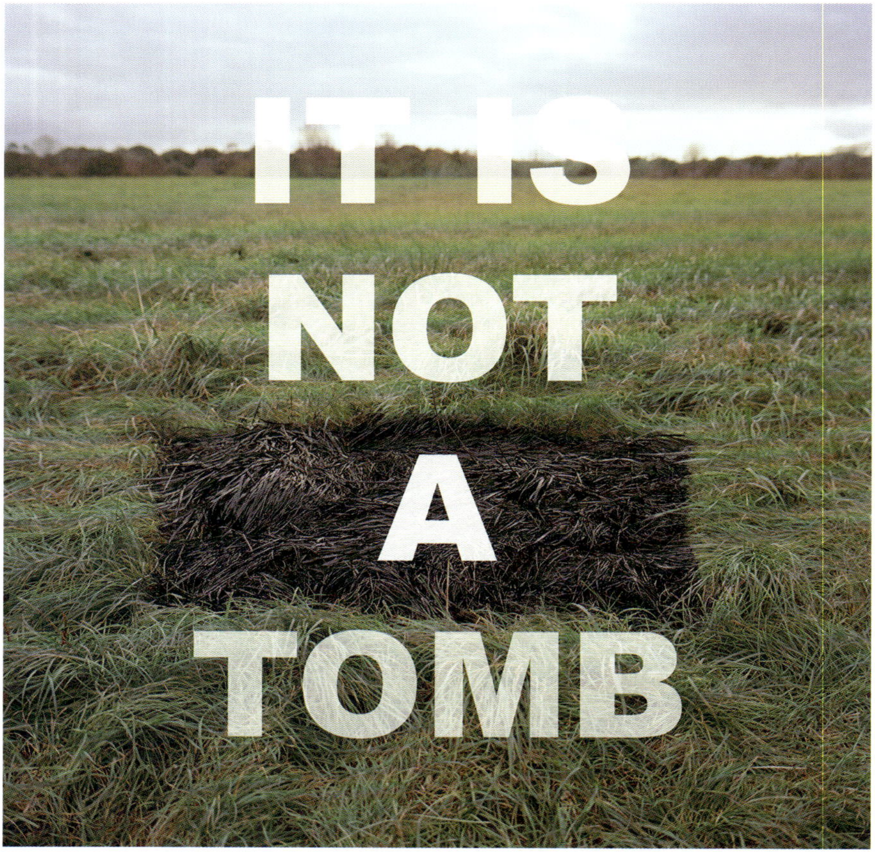
IT IS
NOT
A
TOMB

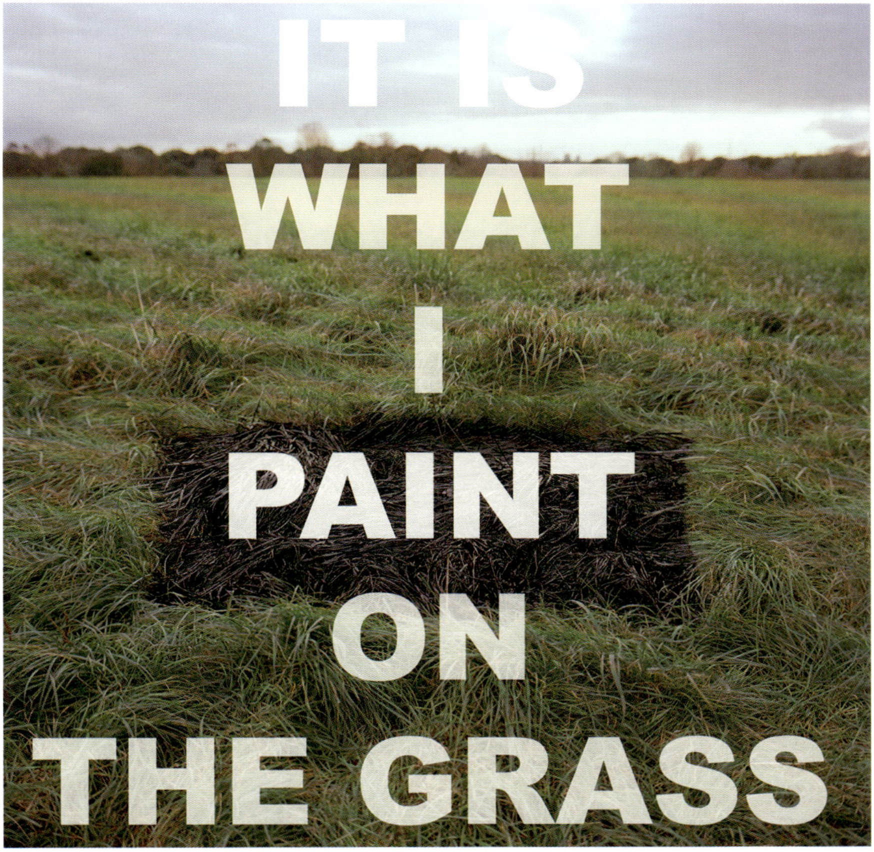
IT IS
WHAT
I
PAINT
ON
THE GRASS

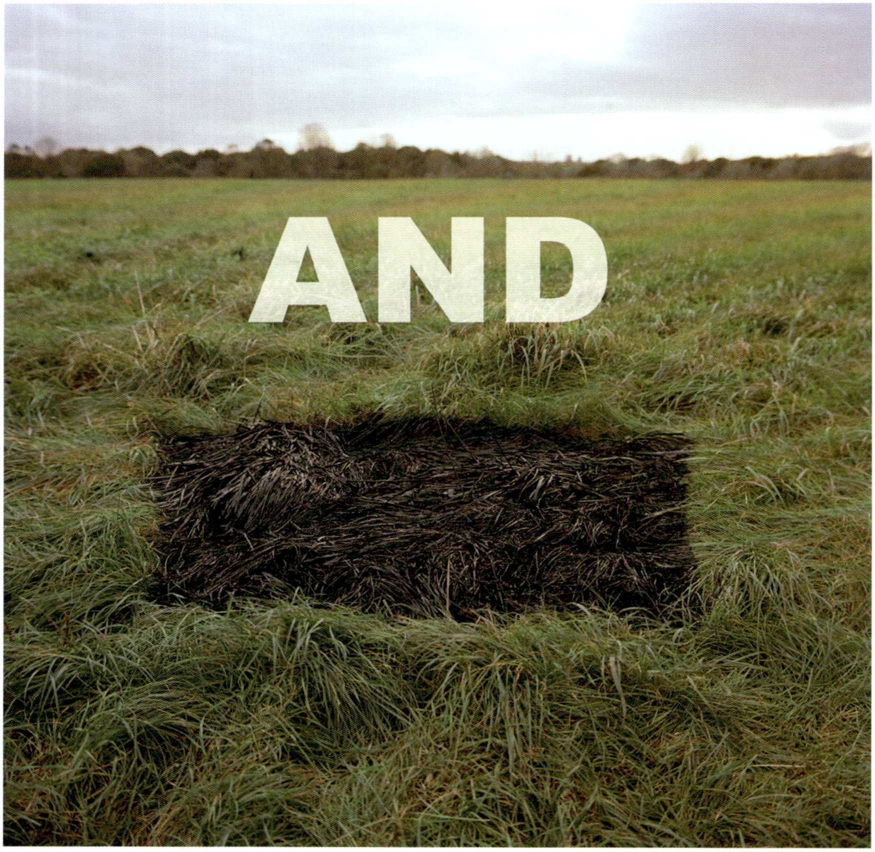
AND

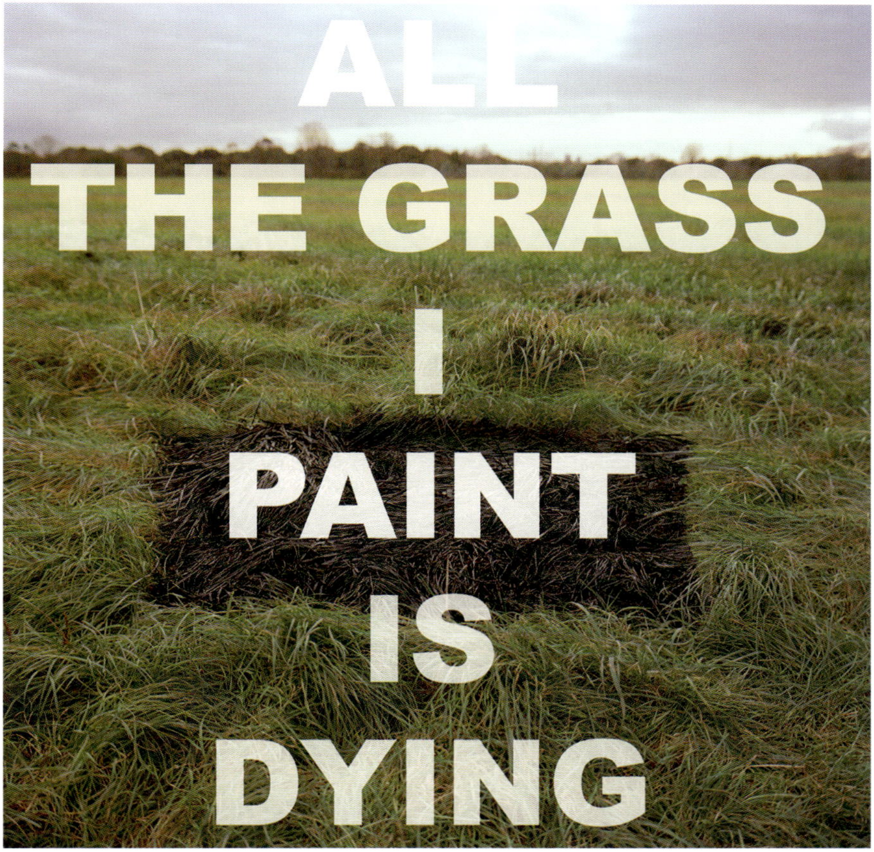
ALL
THE GRASS
I
PAINT
IS
DYING

Creature of Alternative Education,
justify yourself, Debt Keeper

What are you studying?
Business Studies.
AKA the human condition.
I am a survivalist.

Distracted, you see, over your Guru's shoulder, an old flame—they're all here tonight—it was a bad breakup.

Next room.

A room of murals, not quite observed. It is crowded. Faces painted red and glittering.

Overhearing—*I don't know how much I believe in art education. I believe in art-history education. Don't tell anybody what art is, tell them what other people have done.*

Can't we look at the work? Isn't that what we're here for?

Soon, says your Guru. *First, I want you to meet someone. You're familiar with Lawrence Weiner?*

Entering the conversation, a man with a beard—*If you have a Master's degree in anything, you have to write a research paper in another language than your own. They want to accredit one of the last professions that you don't need a license in order to do.*

Is this really him?

A teacher is a very dedicated, really involved human being. The only trouble is, in order to do their job correctly, they have to assume authority. As an artist, I chose a long time ago to try to not have to assume authority.

Something draws you to him. Just as you get close, the statement—

And then he bummed her in his fucking Vauxhall.

Women, men. Short skirts, tight suits.

One storms off.

One calls after—*Phil, when was the last time you licked her fanny?*

Another—*He's fuming. Look at him, he's a fucking cunt.*

Too coarse and out of character. This must not be pretend. Every now and then—

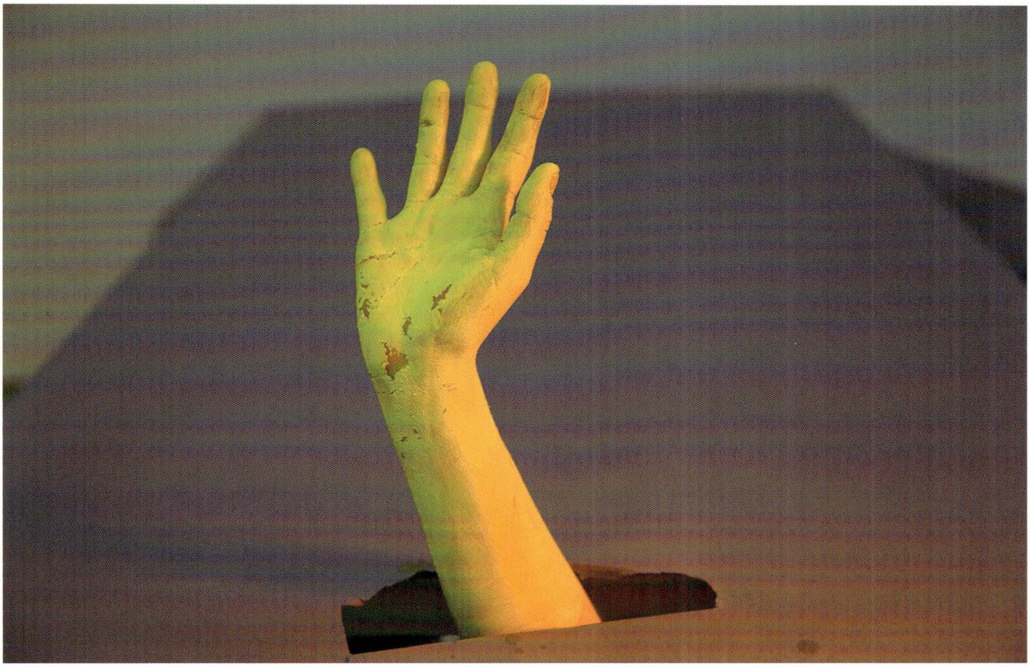

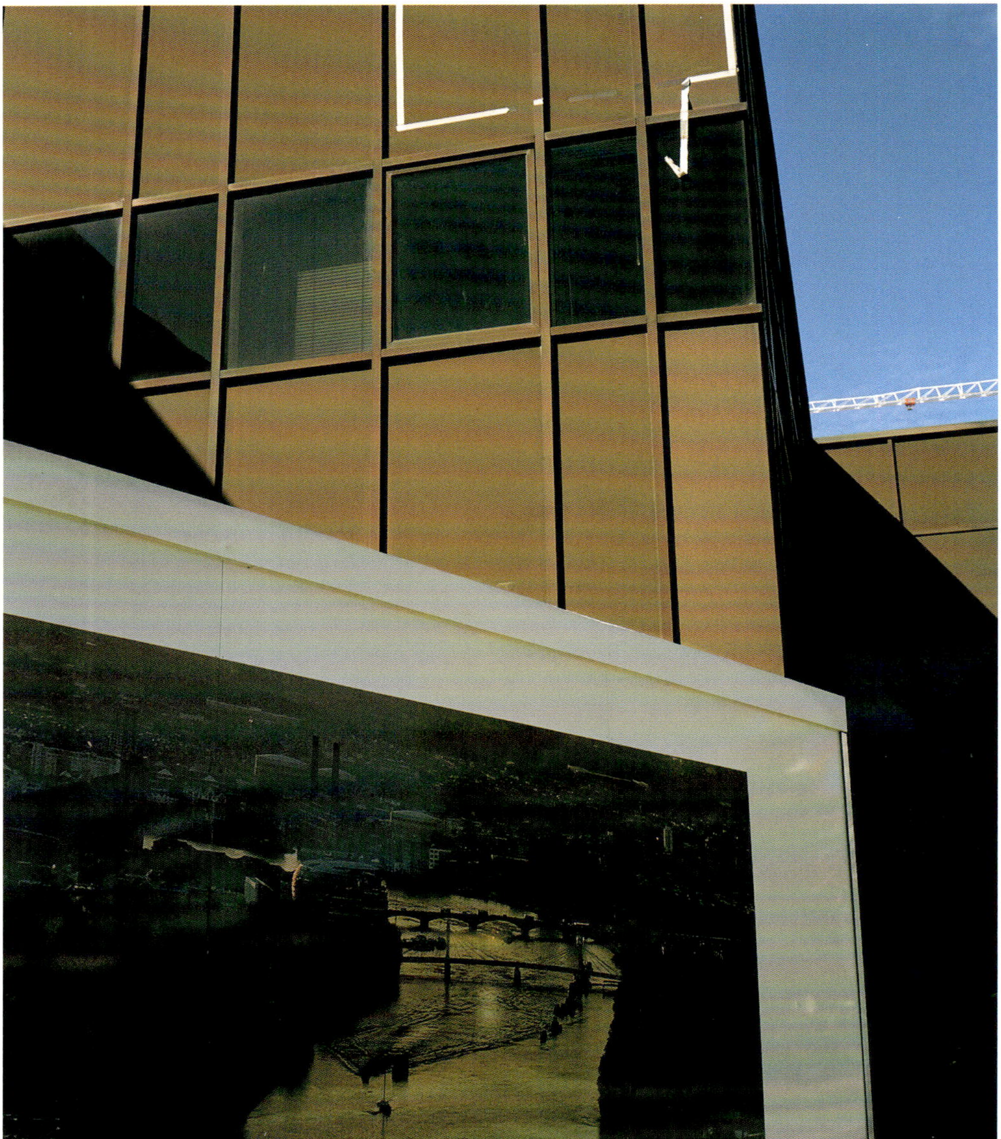

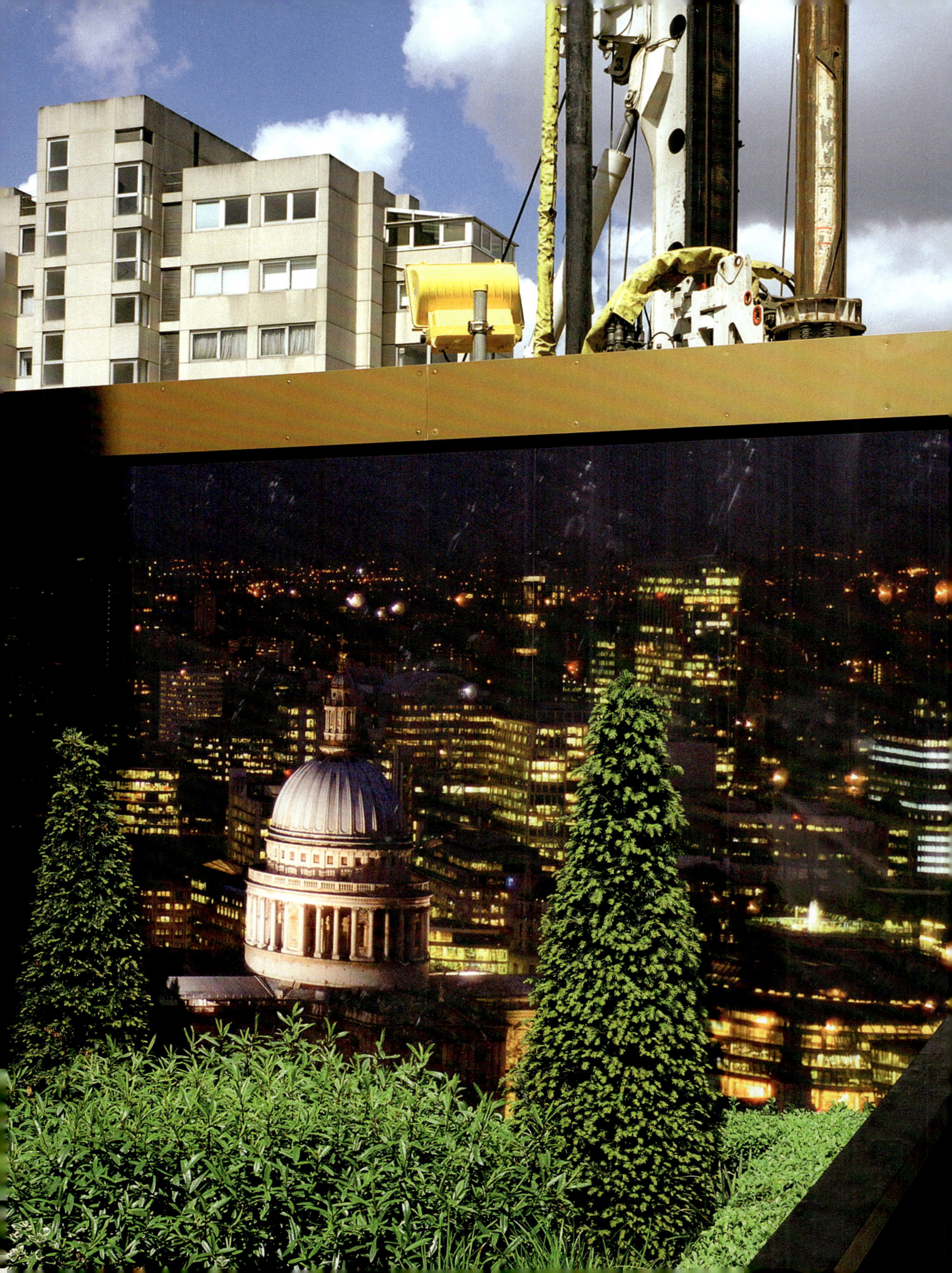

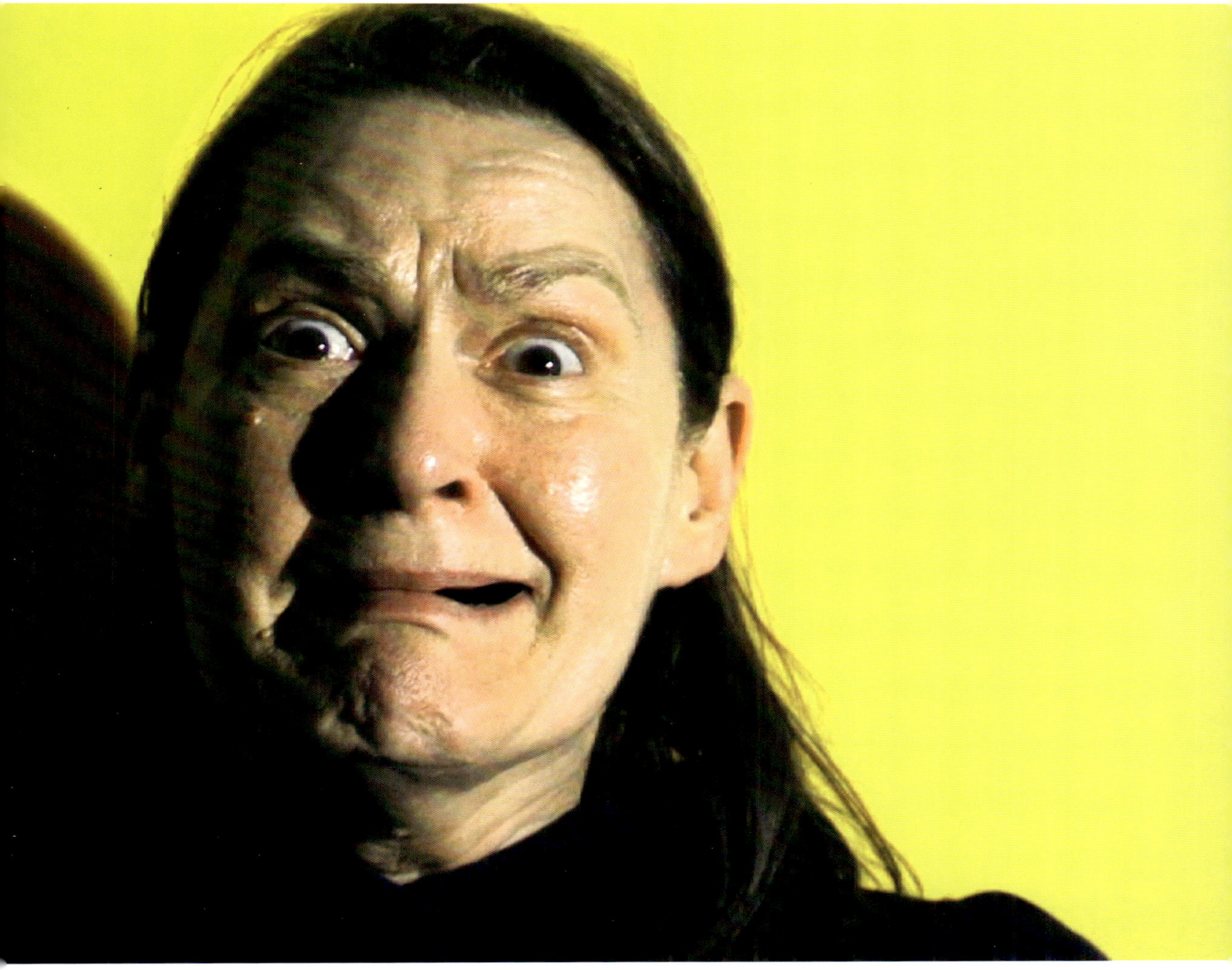

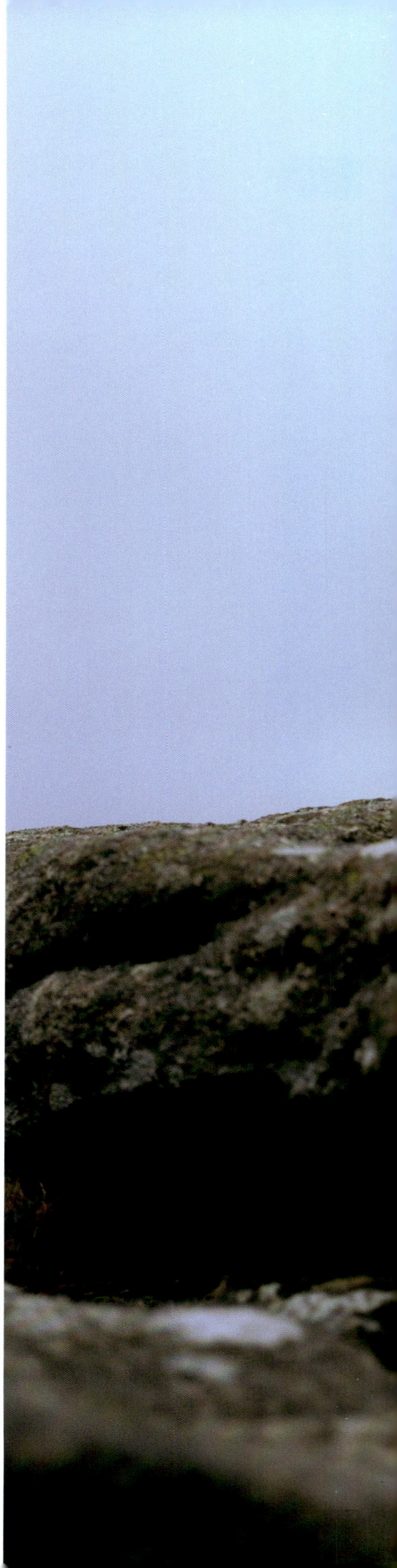

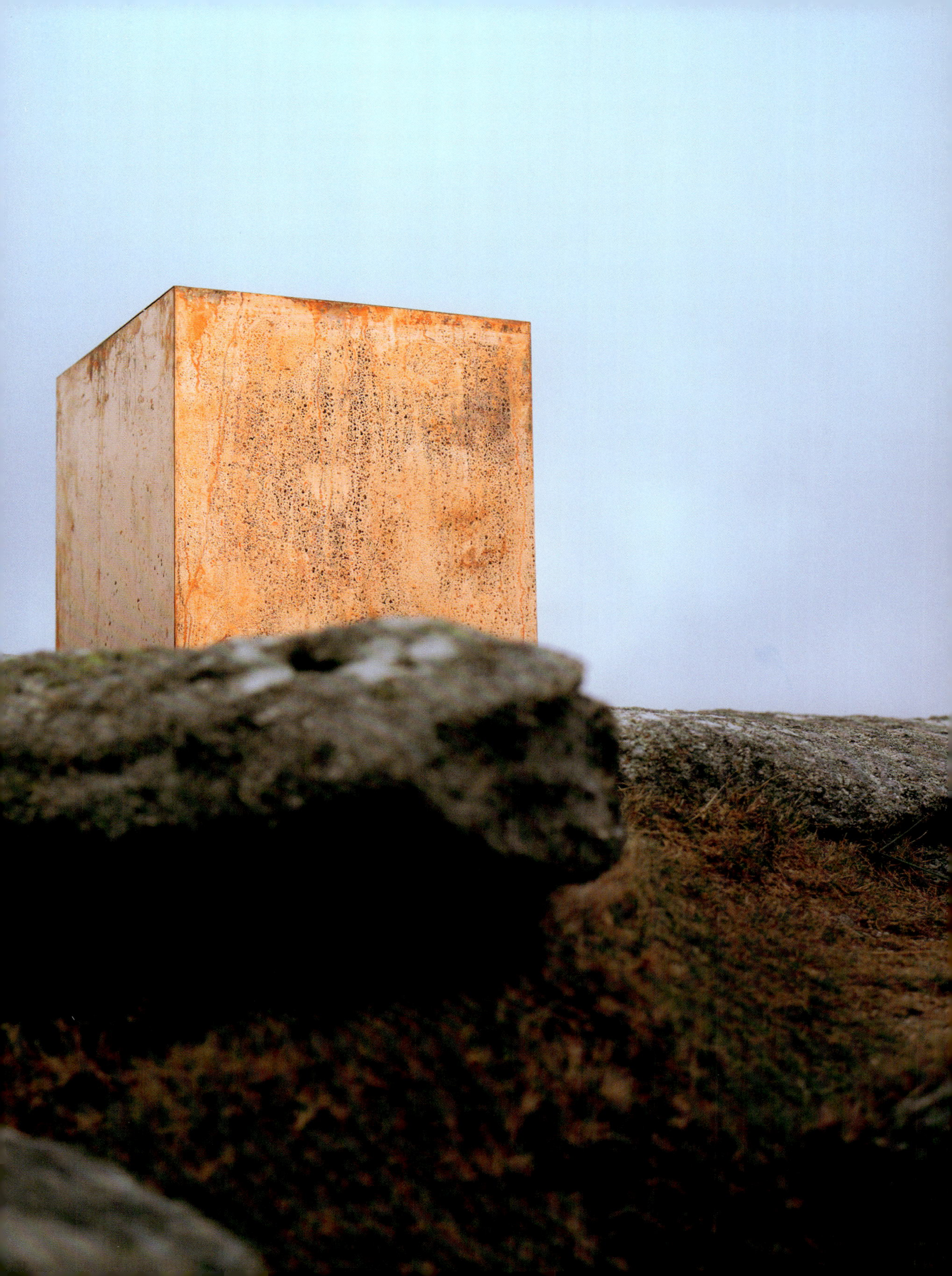

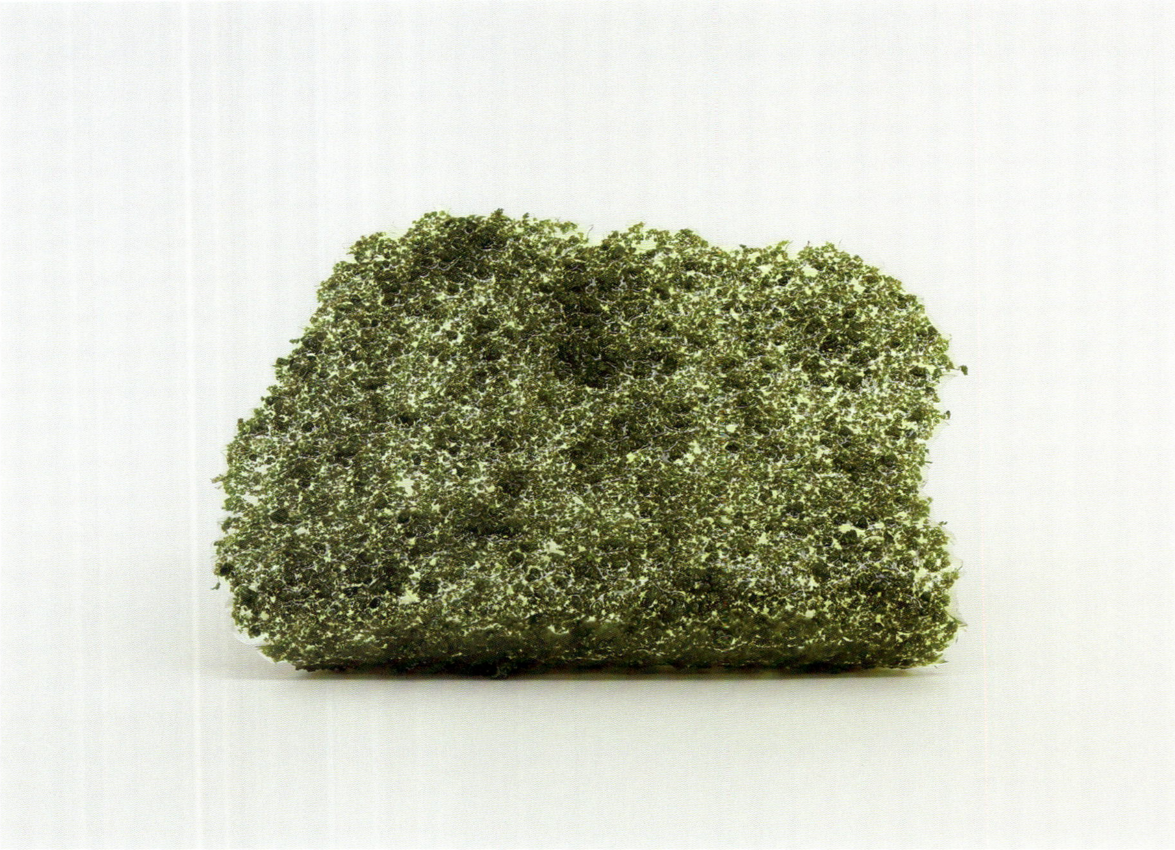

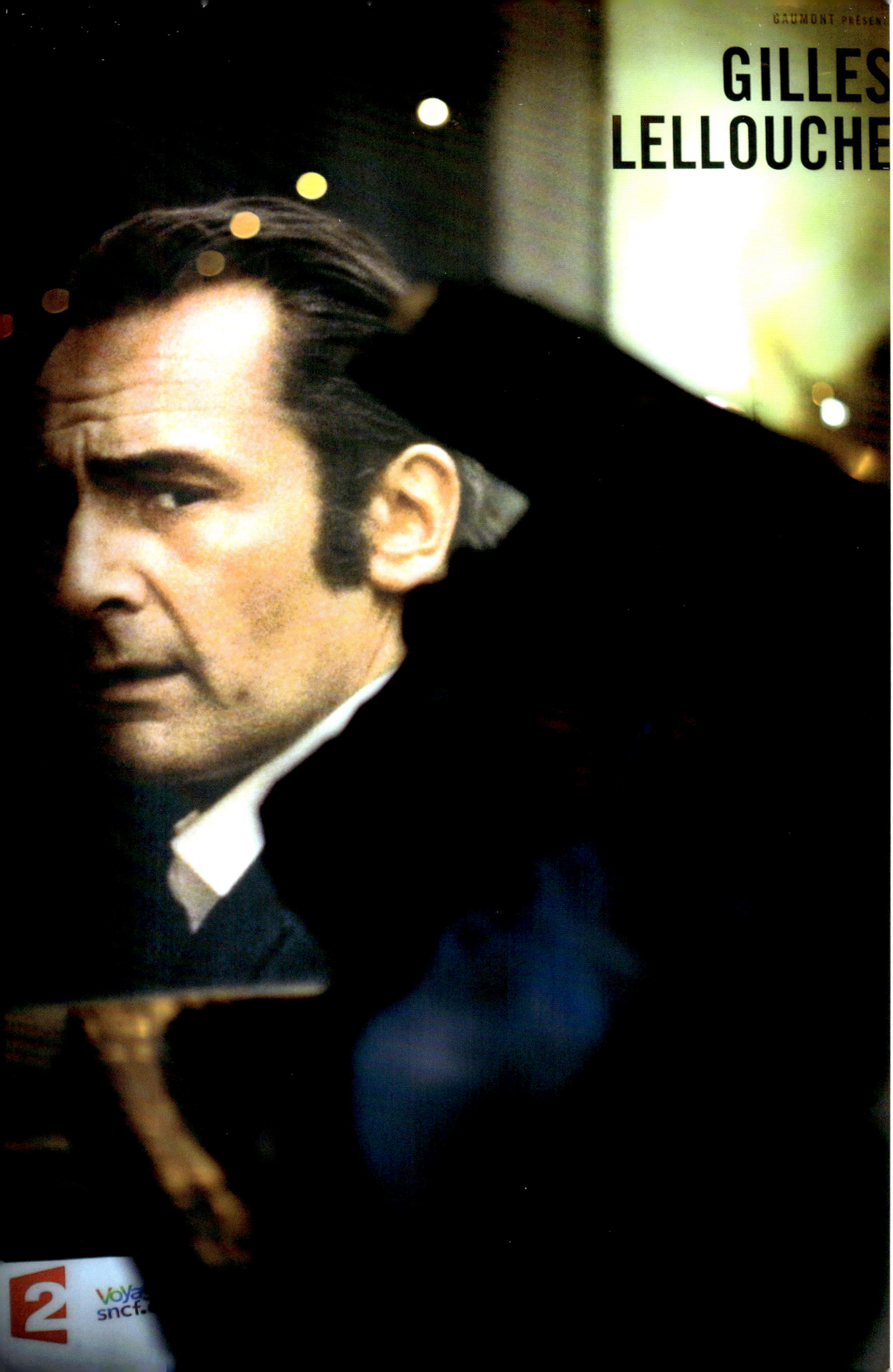
GAUMONT
GILLES
LELLOUCHE

Shame on you.

The Official Photographer pushes through. *The Duke of Bedford is here*, she hisses. *The Duke of Bedford is here.*

The Duke of Bedford?

Codeword for cocaine, says your Guru, again with that smile. Sharing a look, dramaturgically you are placed lowly.

You follow.

Crowded in an office, drawing lines on a glass desk. Your Guru laughs. The lines disappear.

Back outside, there is that couple, still arguing.
Girl—*I am trying to understand you.*
Boy—*You shouldn't need to try. Love doesn't try.*
Girl—*Then how can I tell you what I don't know?*
Boy—*Honesty.*

Are our stories honest? your Guru muses. *Inspired by folklore, consumerism, nationhood, fuel, I am interested in your voice.*

I like art but I want personal and unique experiences and I never feel like art gives me that.

You want?

To be the only one who sees what I see.

An exclusive relationship.

You are not going to believe who's just walked in...

Chris Martin

You wish you could ask—*Were you ever alone at the end of the night carrying a guitar and amp at Kilburn Station after a show waiting for a train to take you home, wondering why you do what you do?*

I can't go back, you say.

Which is when you are led.

See that door. Go to it. Pull back the curtain. Don't be frightened. I'm right behind you.

A man running, an arrow, an open door.

Its green light dims, slowly, and very there, in dark, a blue projected. White words NO SIGNAL. Loud speaker relaying human screams.

Speak quietly of art, plucked from the realm—*If this is the home of art, it is a house of horrors.*

The grandchildren

Just a voice—*You find comfort in walls. Rooms, yellowed papers, paper weights. Books leather-bound, pipe tobacco and draped over a chaise longue, a younger lover who chimes, 'Tell me all you know about Giacometti.'*

Empty, bewildered and wanting this to be over.

I can't go back, you repeat, unsure of the meaning in GHOST STORIES.

A lifetime's—*Shame.*

Give me incomplete thoughts and complete adoration.

Out of the dark and into <u>Speeches</u>

Old old
<u>Corrupt Benefactor</u>

Guru—*A practice impossible to legitimise. It is best we not discuss or acknowledge the matter. No good can come of it.*

Live dangerously?
Don't mind if I do, your Guru says, taking a *Trapeze.*

Old old
about to open his mouth—
I promise I won't keep you long. I just want to thank you all for being here in the face of difficult circumstances. By coming tonight we send a clear message. Were those people encountered upon arrival willing to listen, I would tell them this. Ours is the voice of free speech, yours is one of censorship, and as such, you will not be heard.

As he speeches, you and your Guru whisper the following
Let me feel connection.
But how?
Wait until it gets mysterious again.

Is this connection? Or just the twist of emotion, taunting the lonely? *Do you feel maybe we're going off-script?*

Are you deeply in love?

In need of the hard stuff, you answer—*No, but I am looking.*

A man phalanx.

Opprobrium features. Dark suits marching.

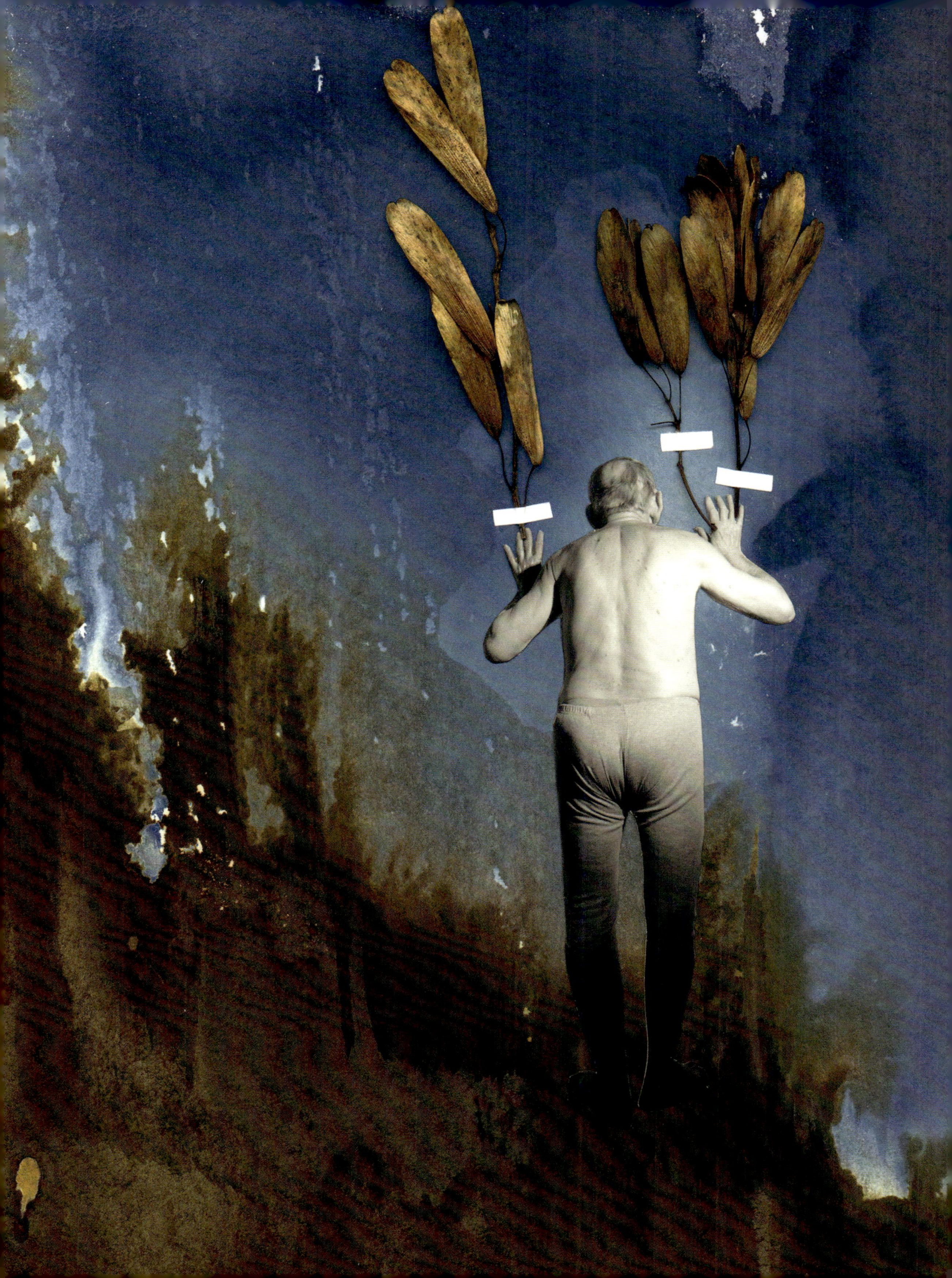

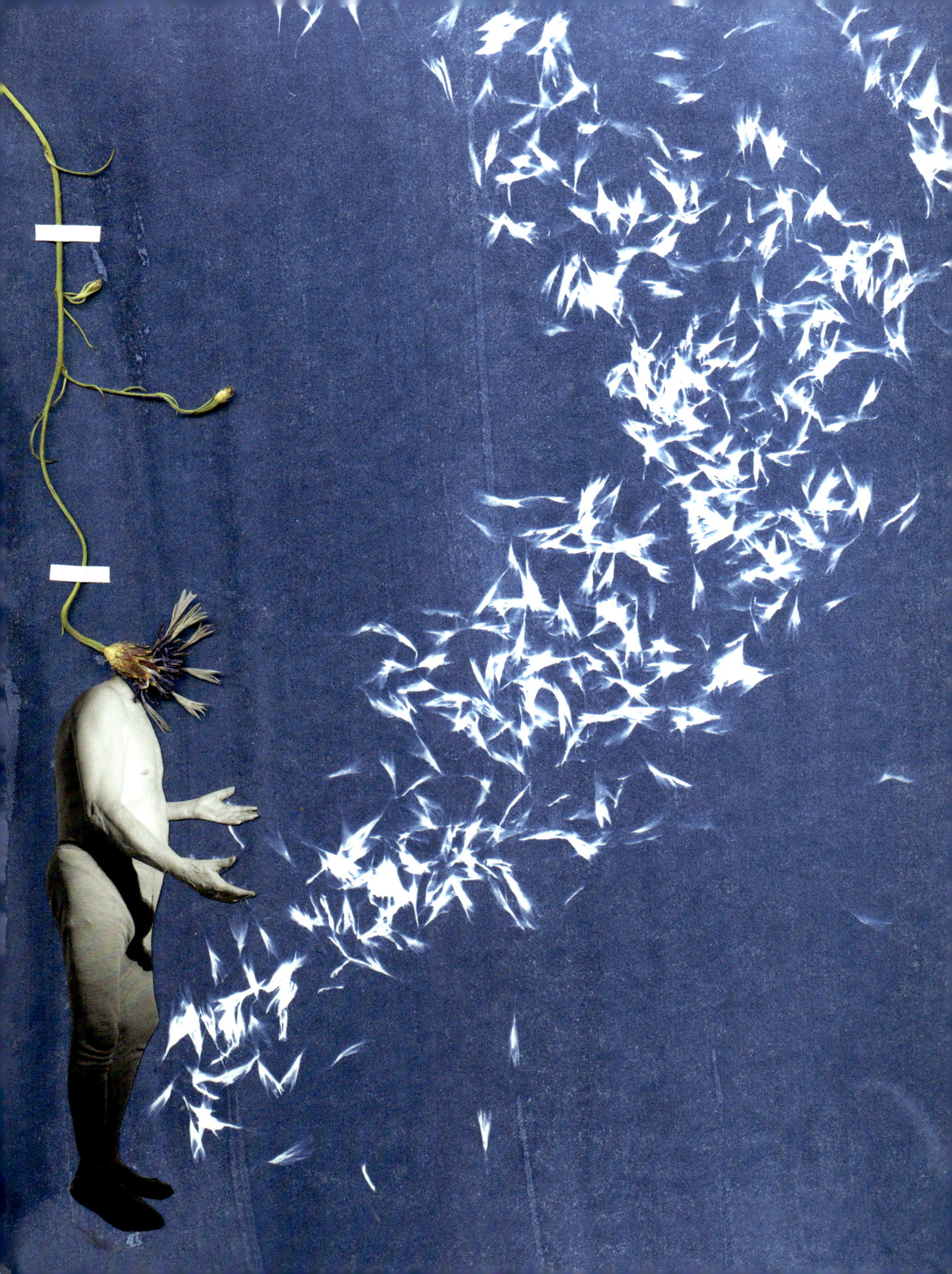

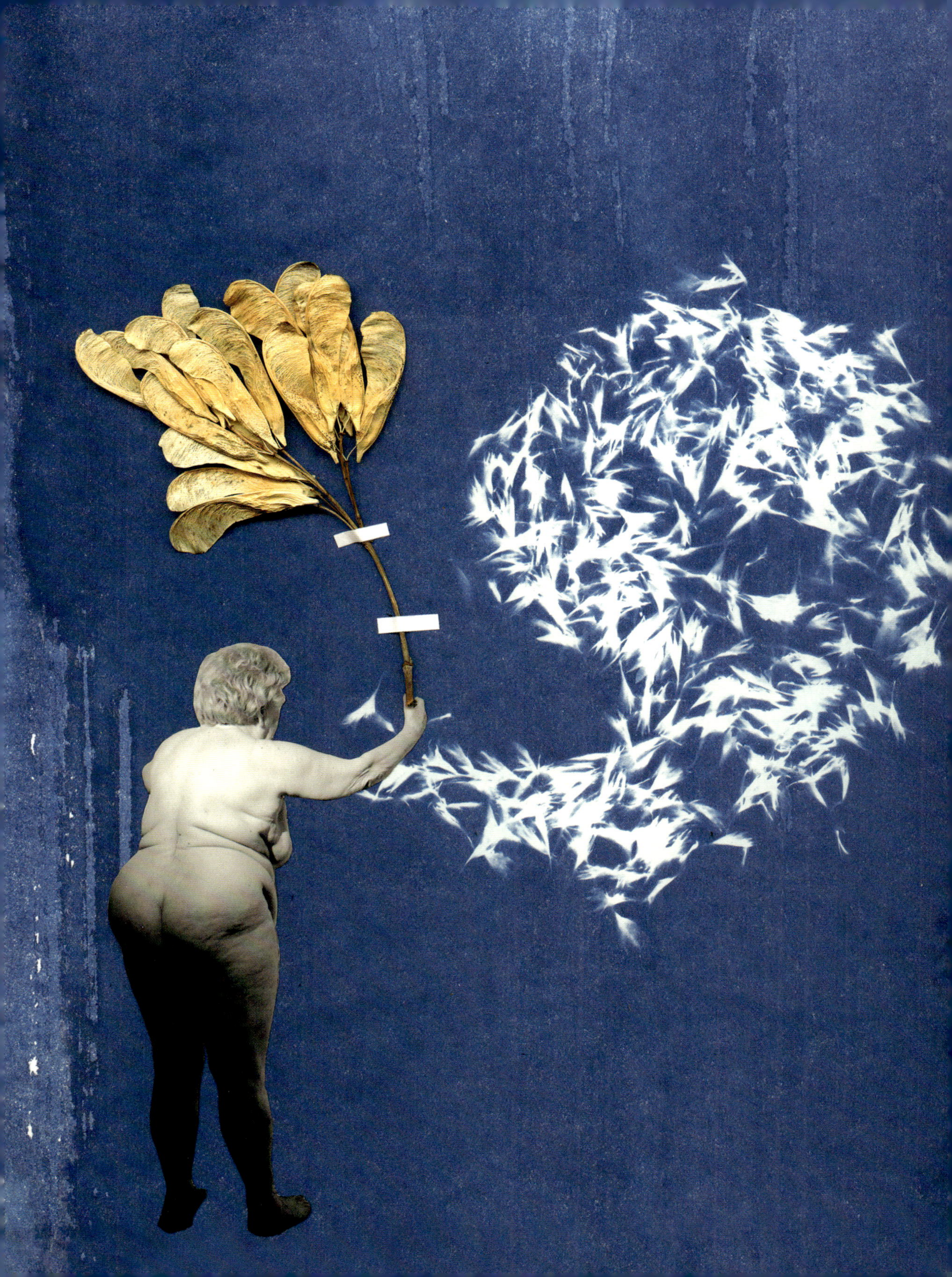

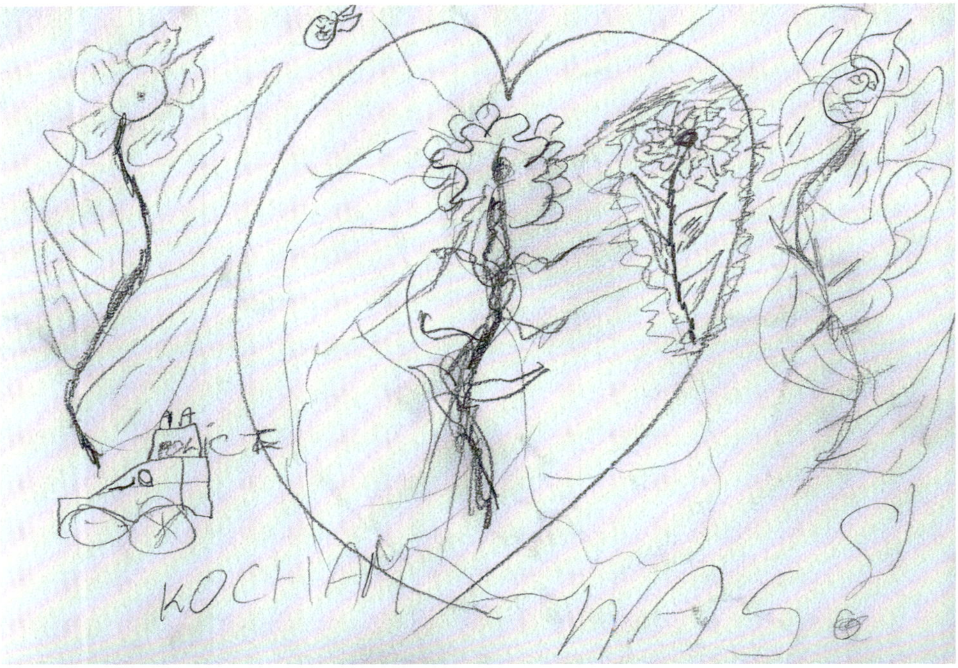
KOCHAM
NAS

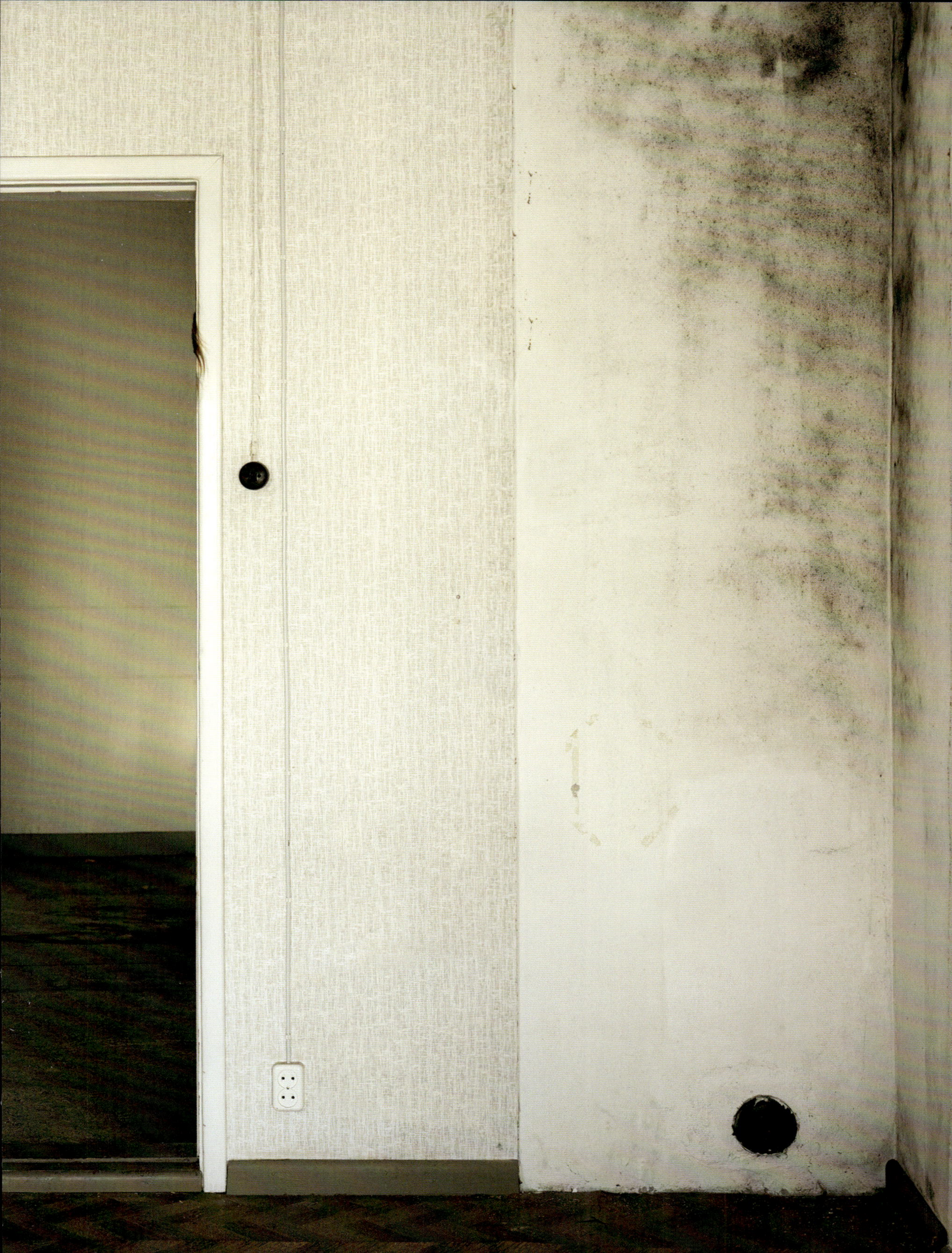

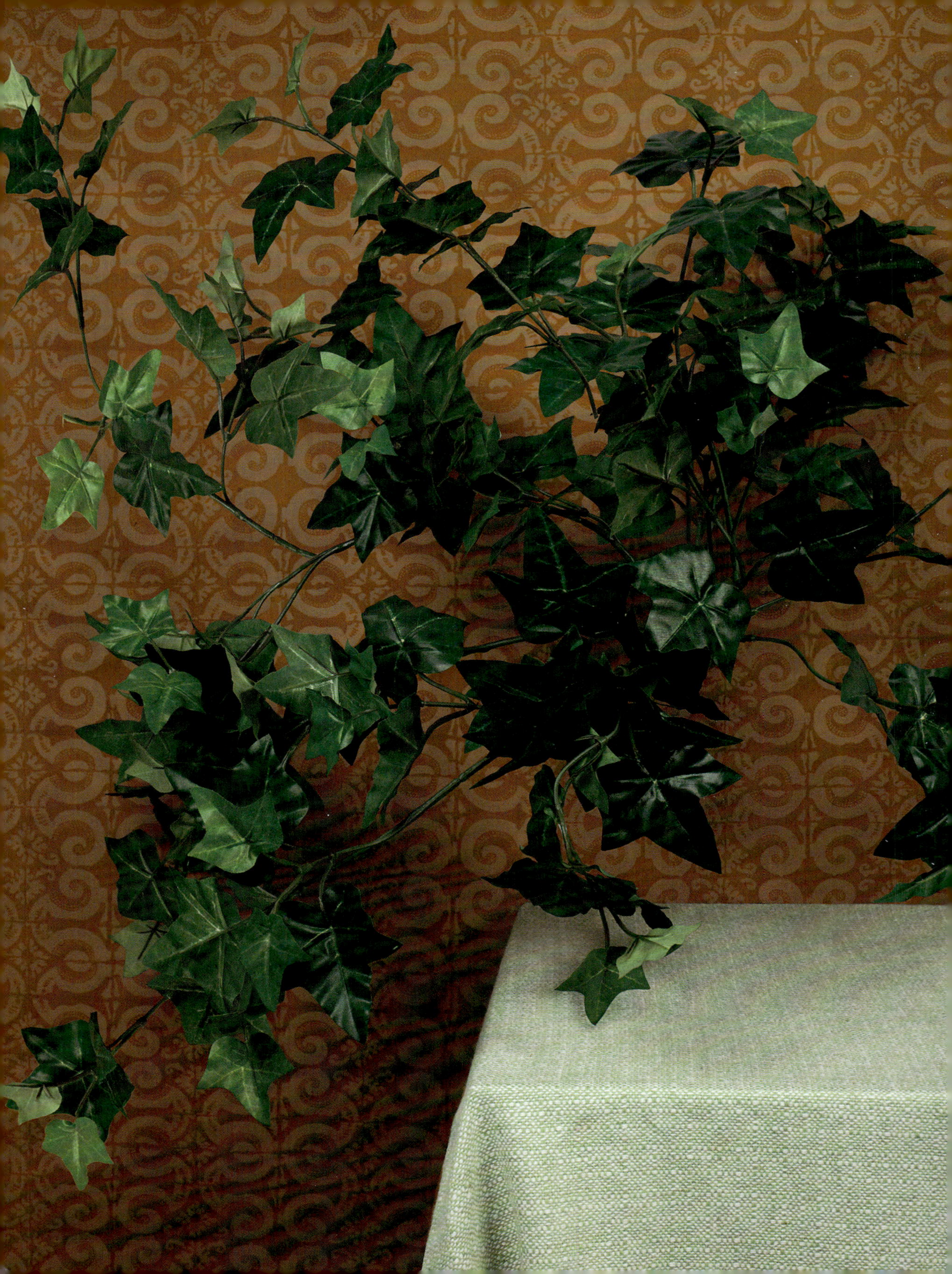

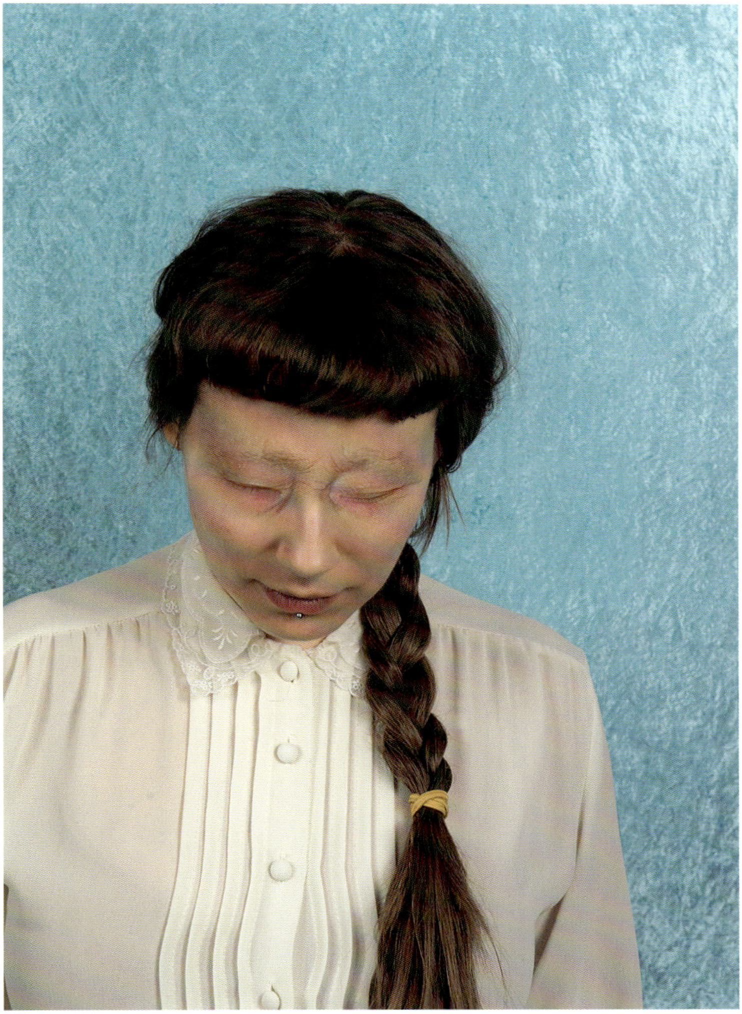

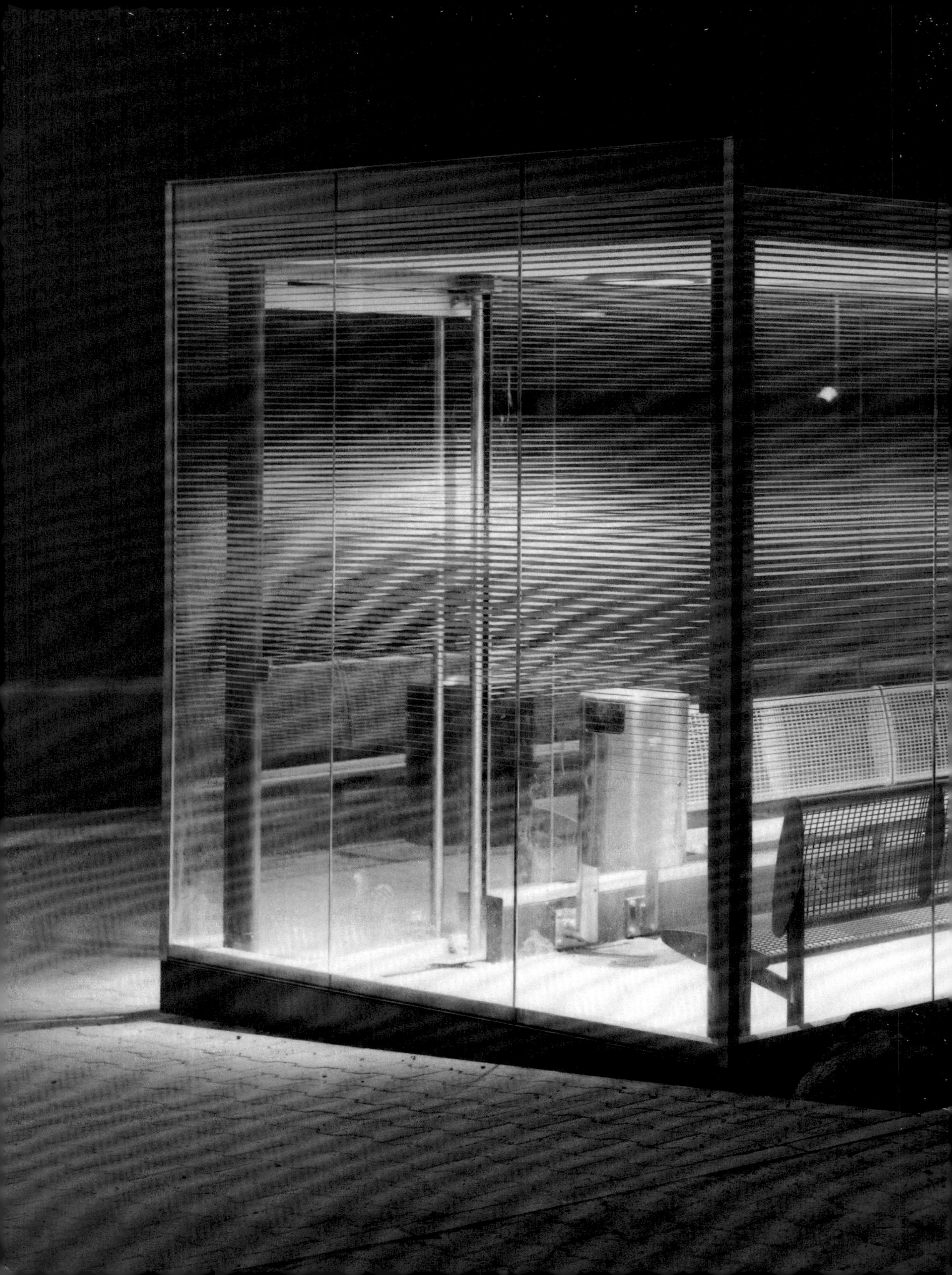

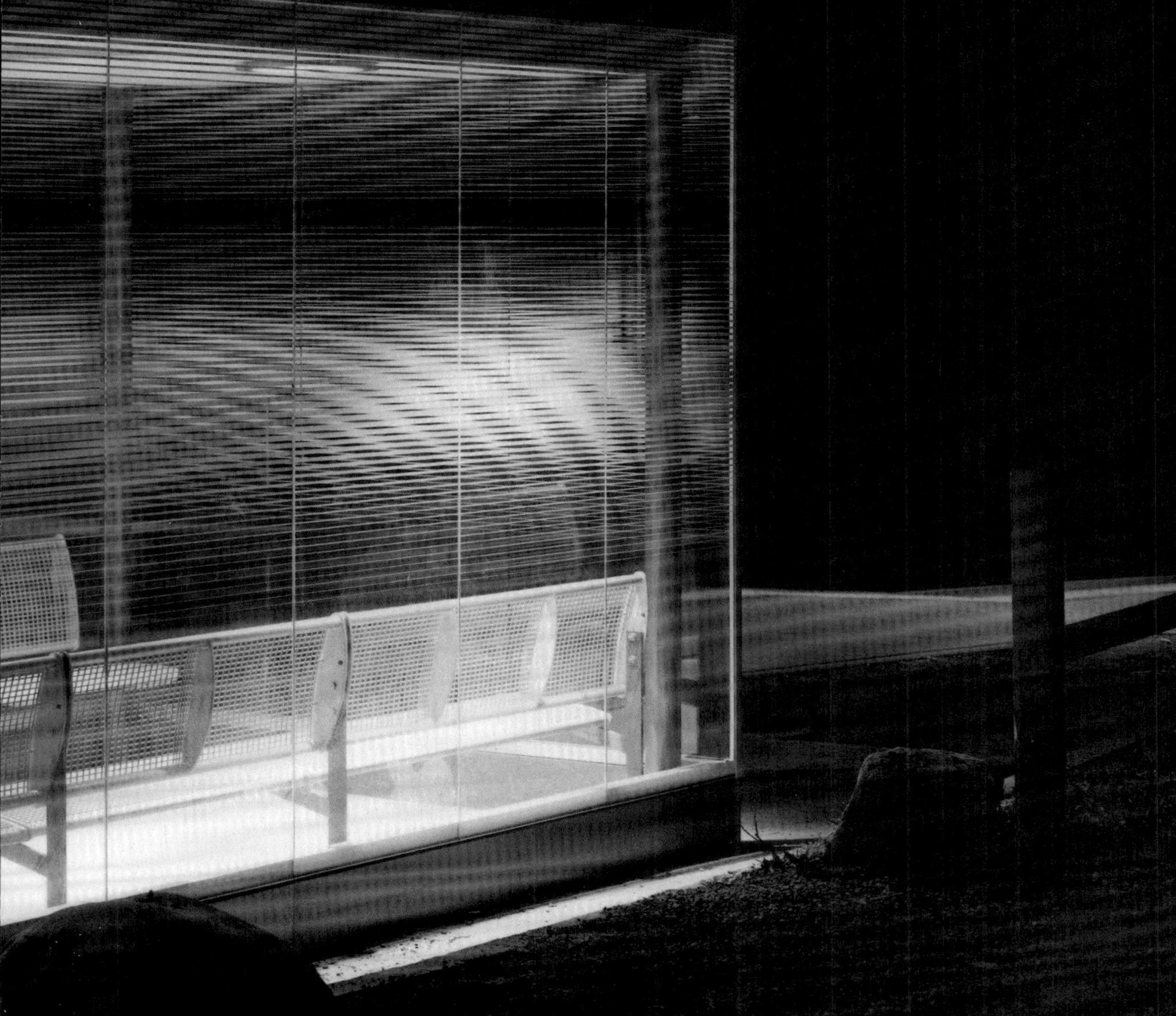

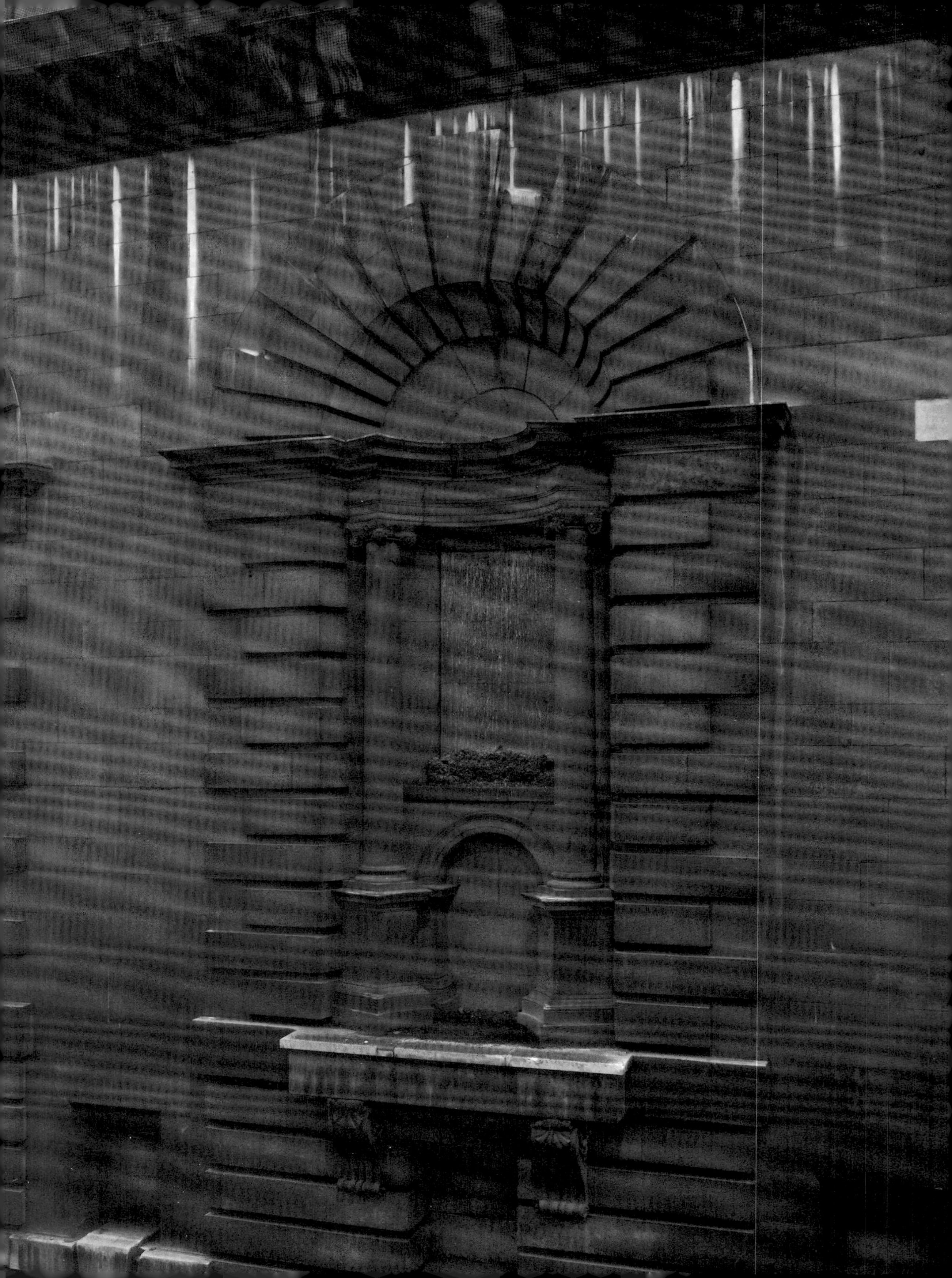

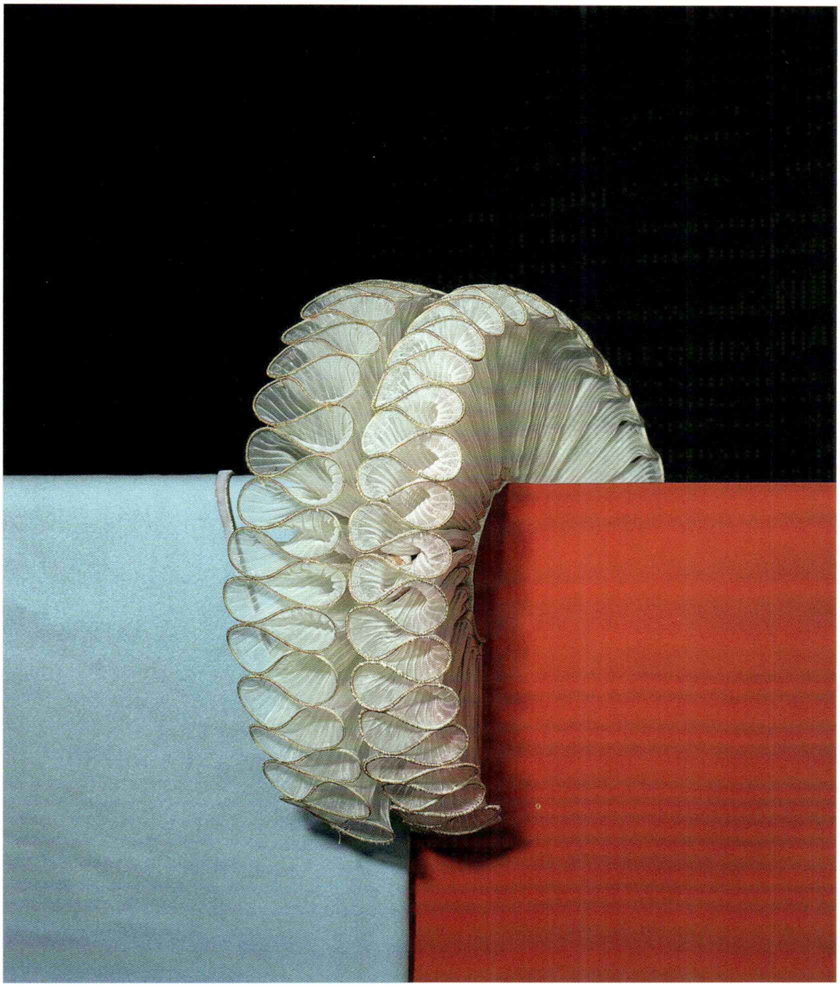

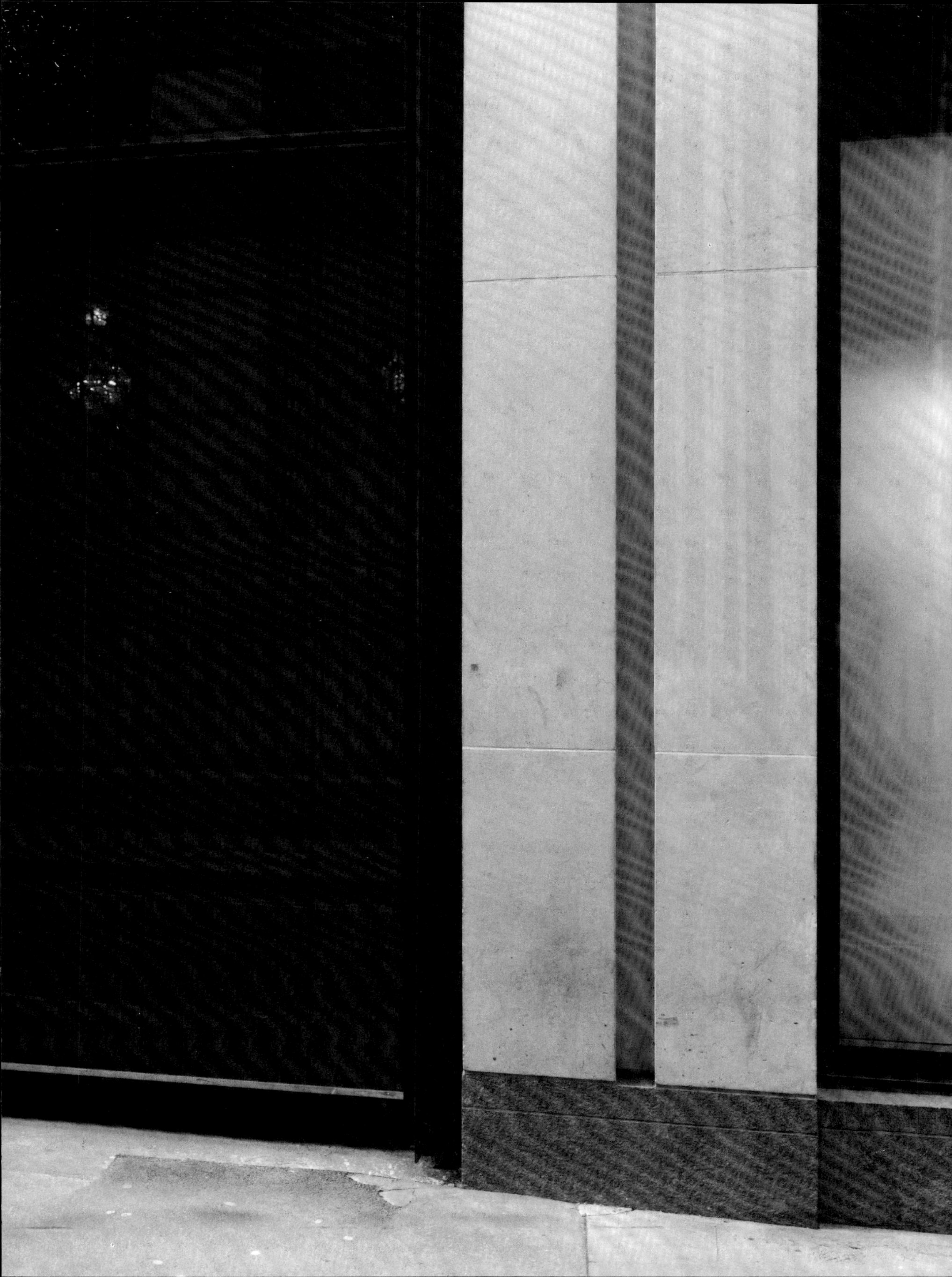

Corrupt

Benefactor

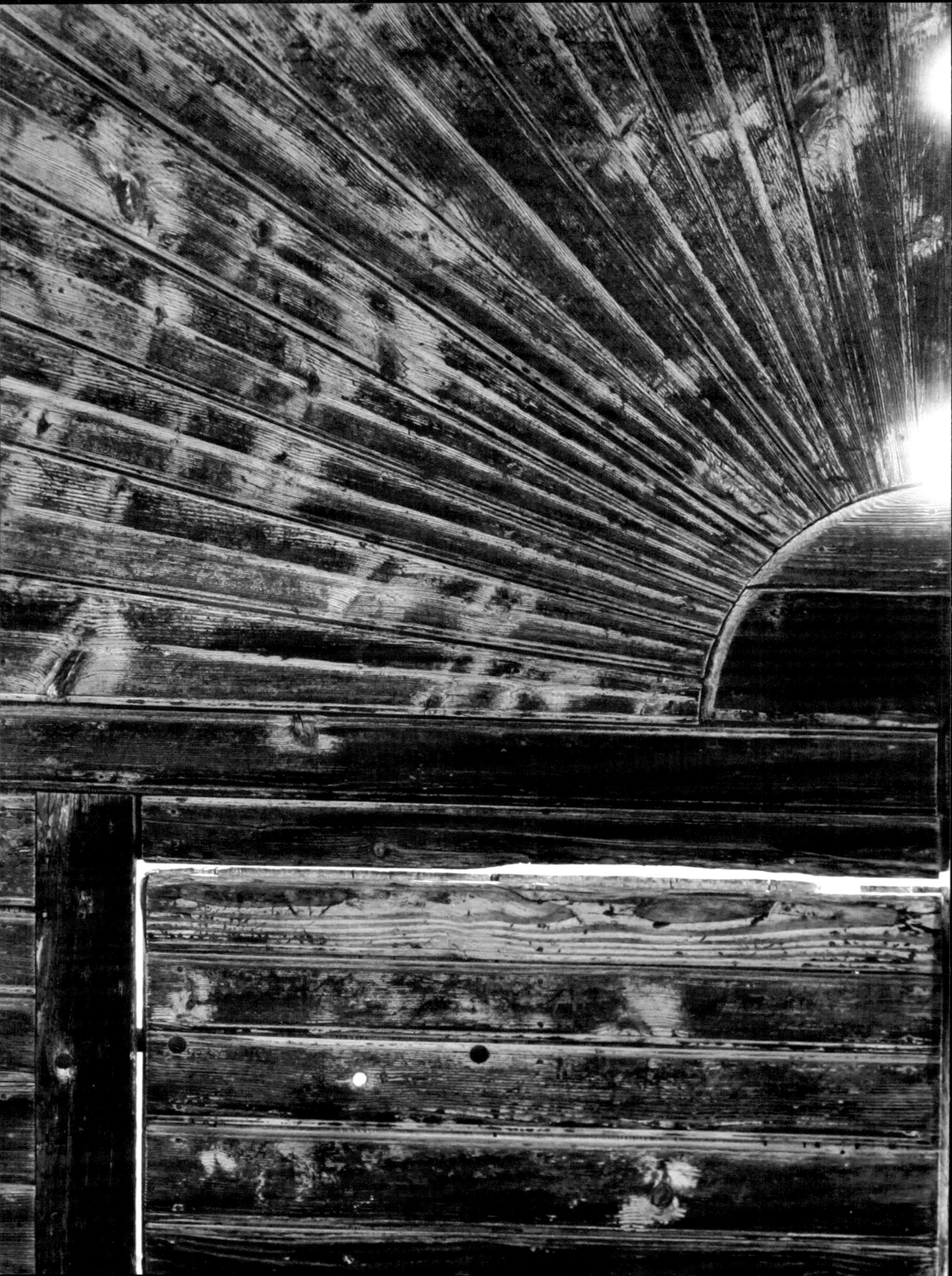

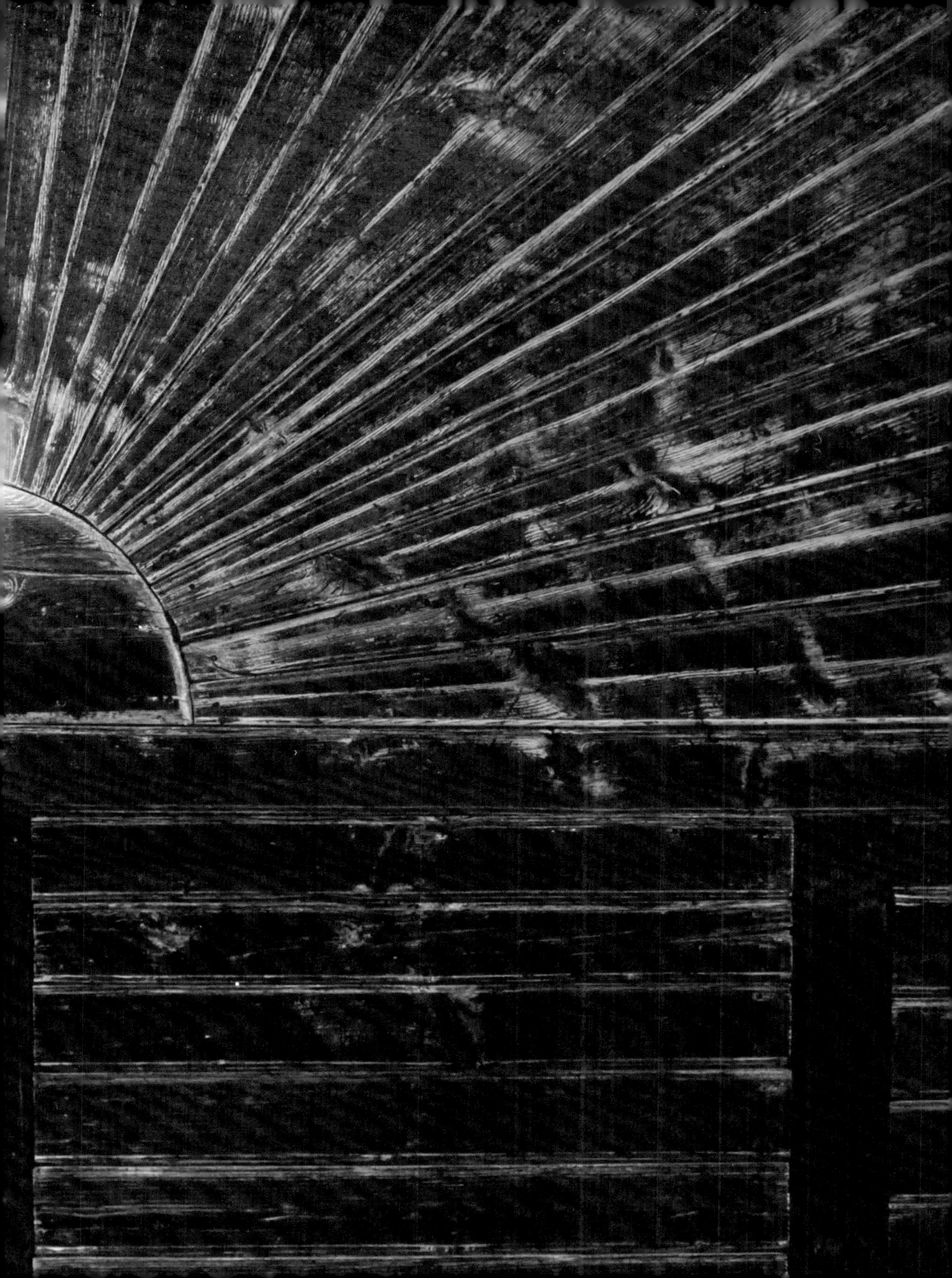

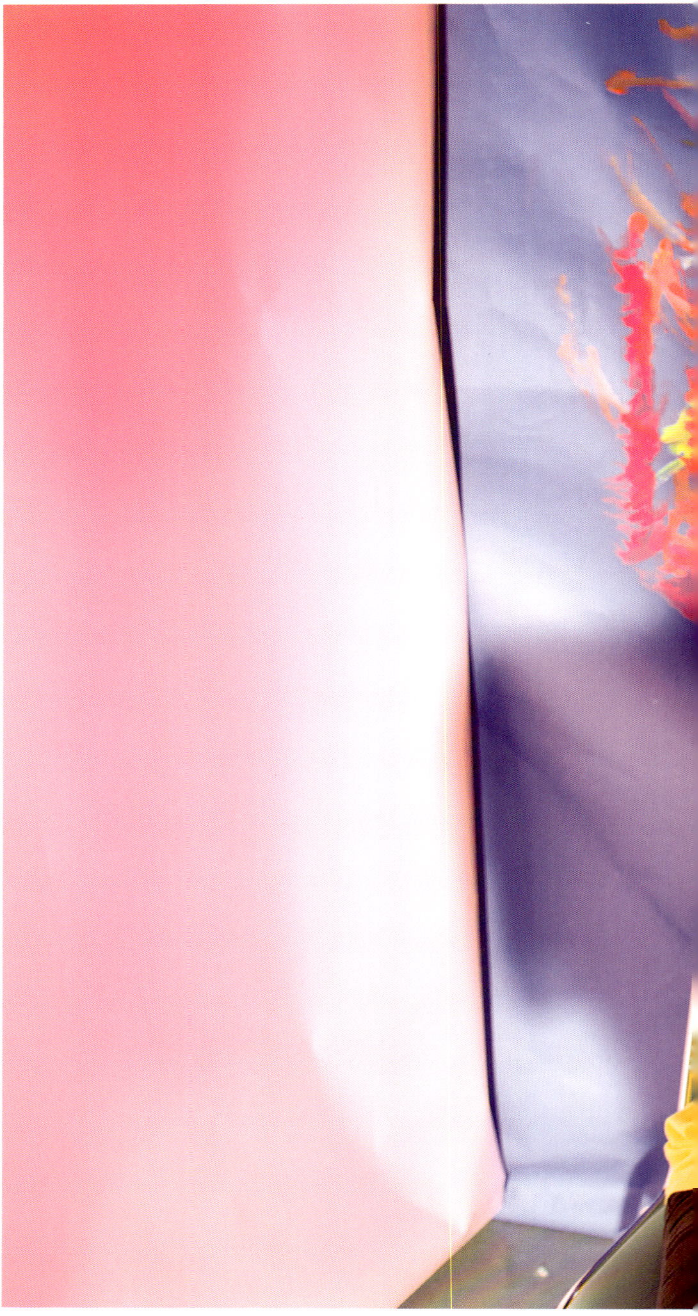

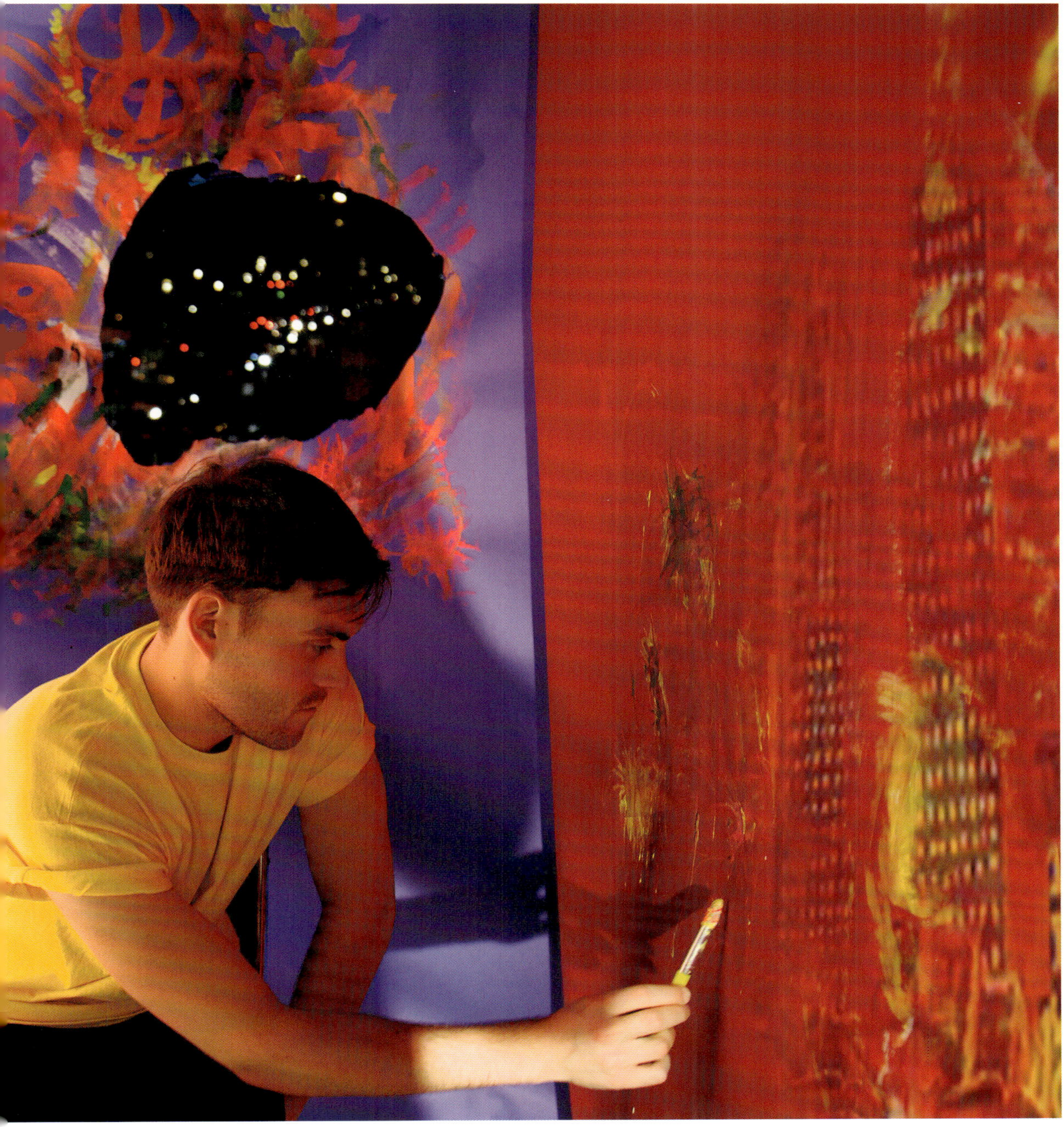

Credit Suisse, whispers your Guru.

Is that a bank?

Not really.

Murmuring—*Credit Suisse*, wondering what they do and what they are doing here.

The men march away, taking your Guru with them.

Alone.

Grows that cry—*Shame on you. You are so far from home*, whispers the wind

Silence mind, give me moments

Next room.

A pram is a plinth holding a baby aloft.

This is an opportunity to see what is on the walls but the pram draws you to it. You peer in.

Flashback: looking into a black hole, waiting for the light of an oncoming train.

Not looking at protestors.

Are you wrong? You did not know you were part of that—repression—yet their message remains—*Shame.*

Can you take comfort in art when you cannot look away from a baby—*I am looking at a mirror that does not look back or tell me anything*—closing your eyes

fluorescents

Are you the artist?

Quizzical expressions. The Official Photographer hands you a card

Every time you start
tell yourself
it has to be big

For the memory of protest, cry.

At the foot of the door, a stainless steel bowl. Inside it is something green. *Trapeze*? Reminding you of a night this once was.

Now come phantom vibrations at your thigh—where your phone should be—*phibrations*—as if it seeks to tell you something. Your phone wants to give you a warning.

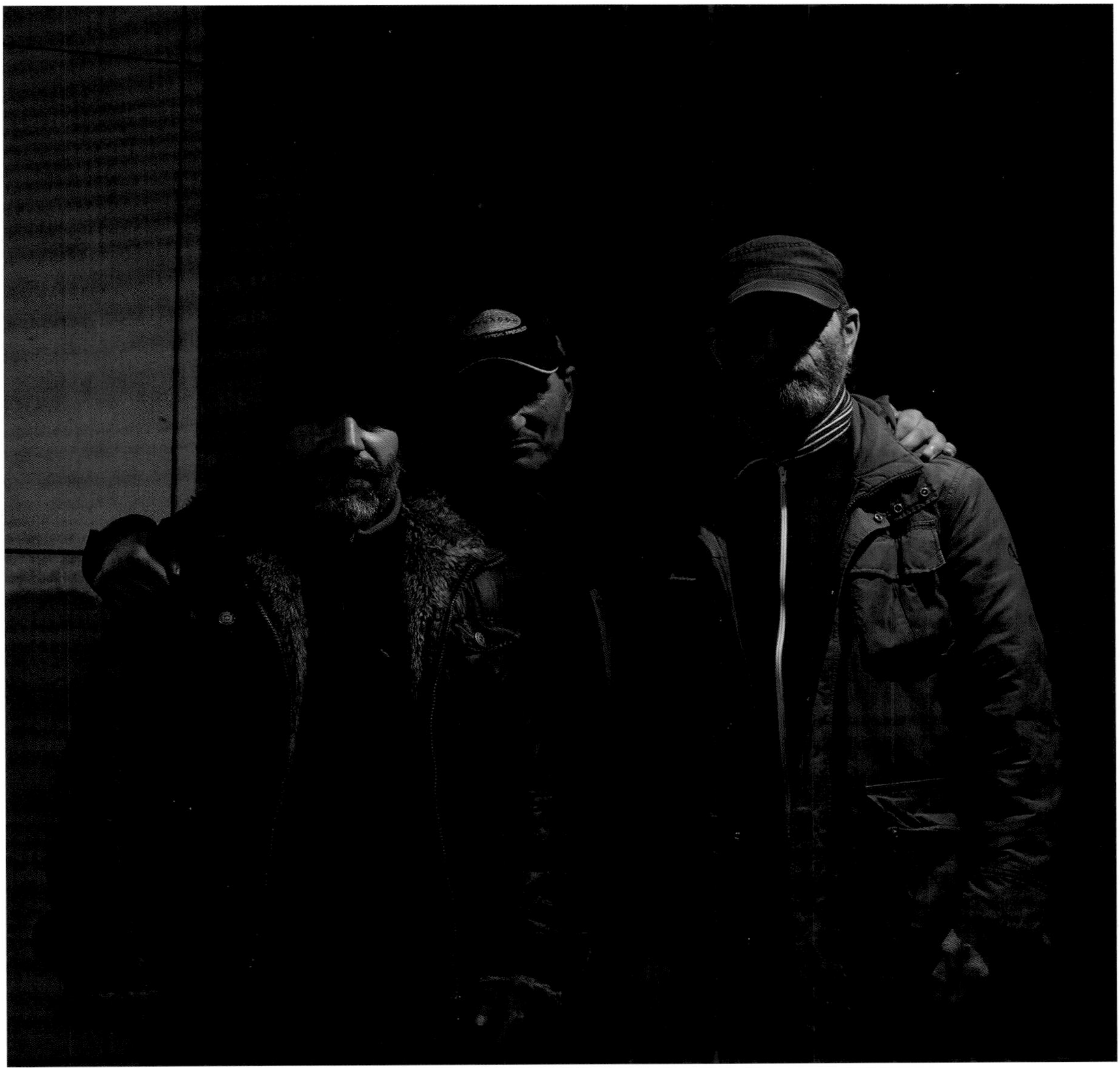

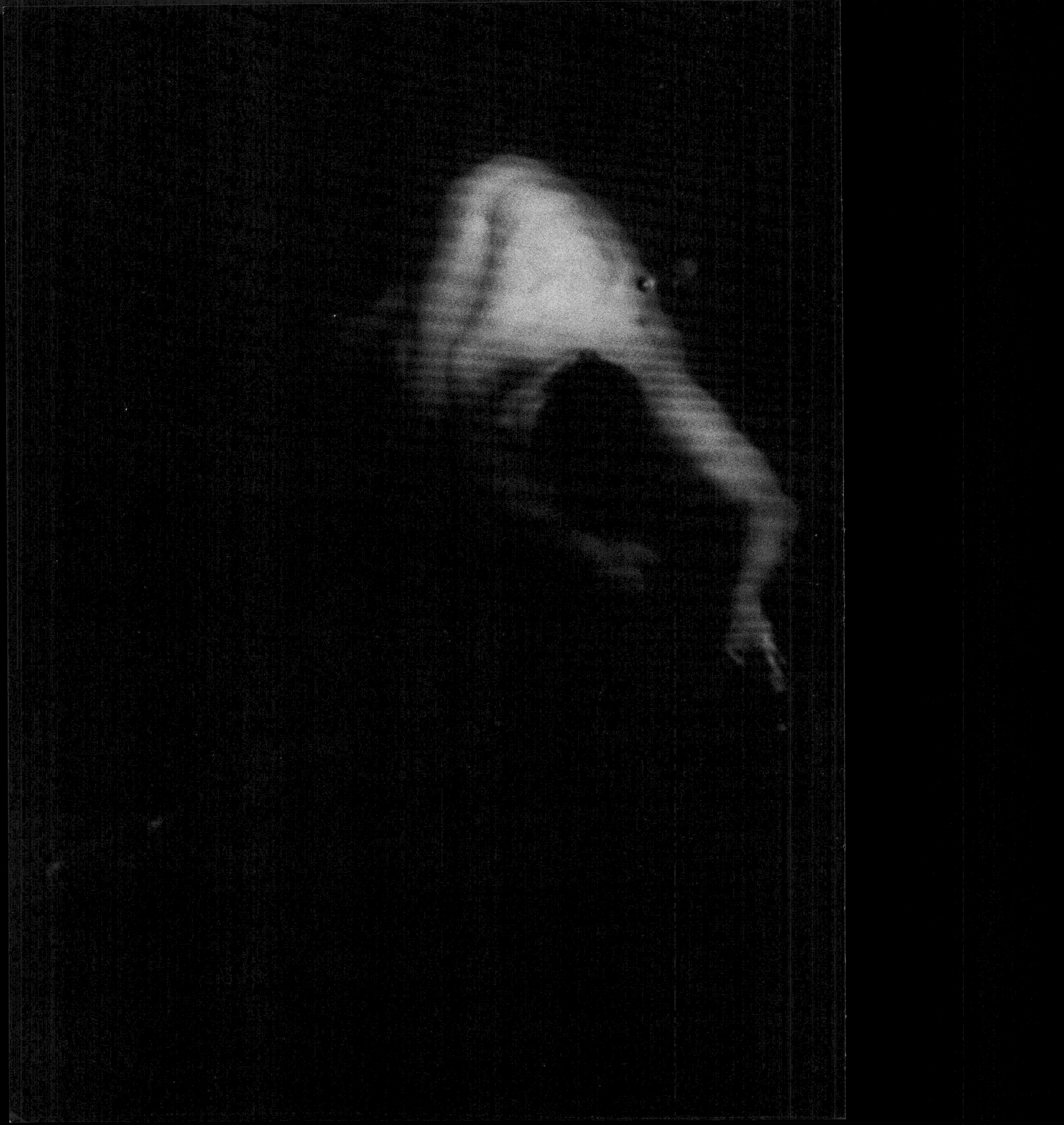

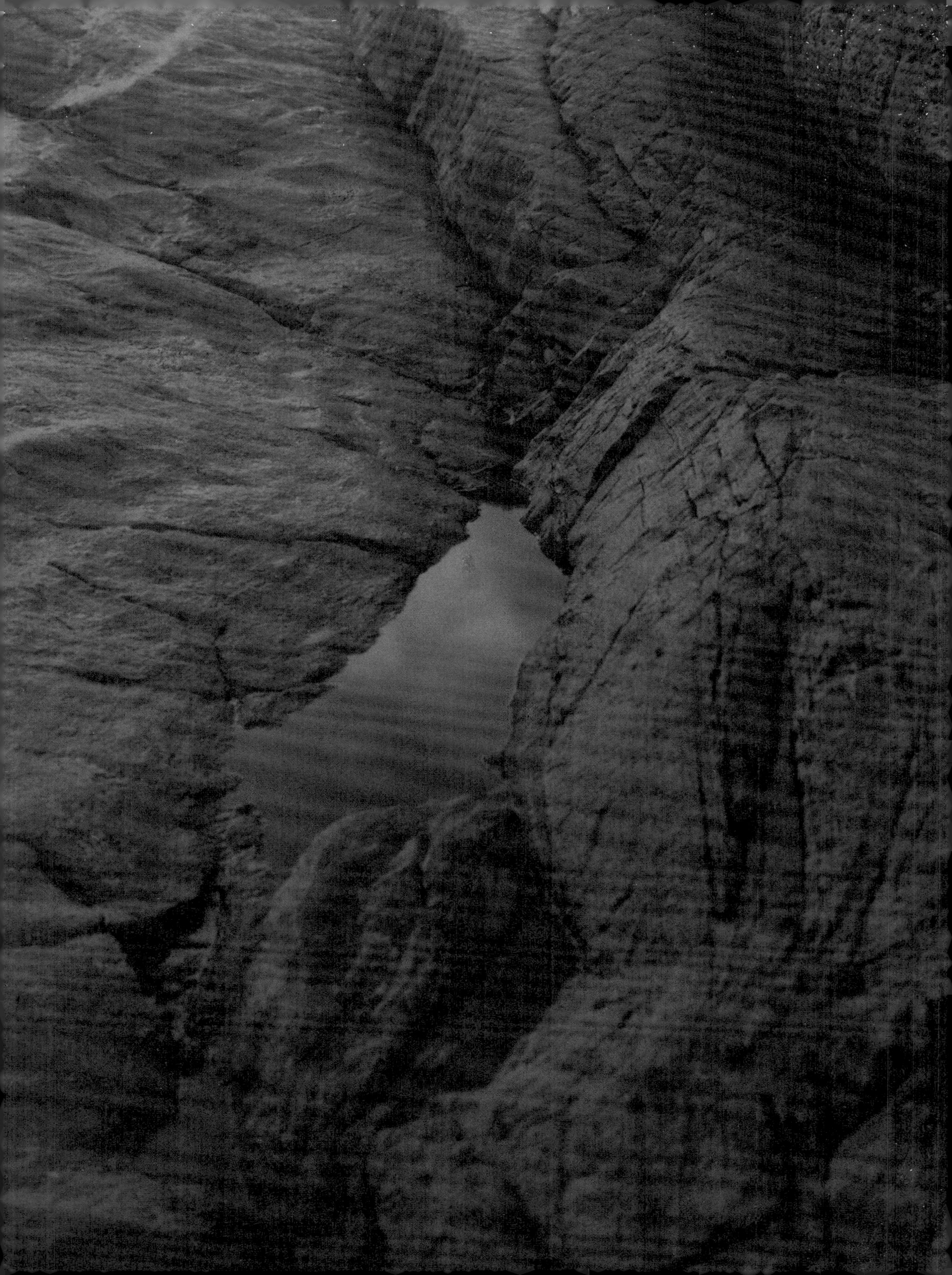

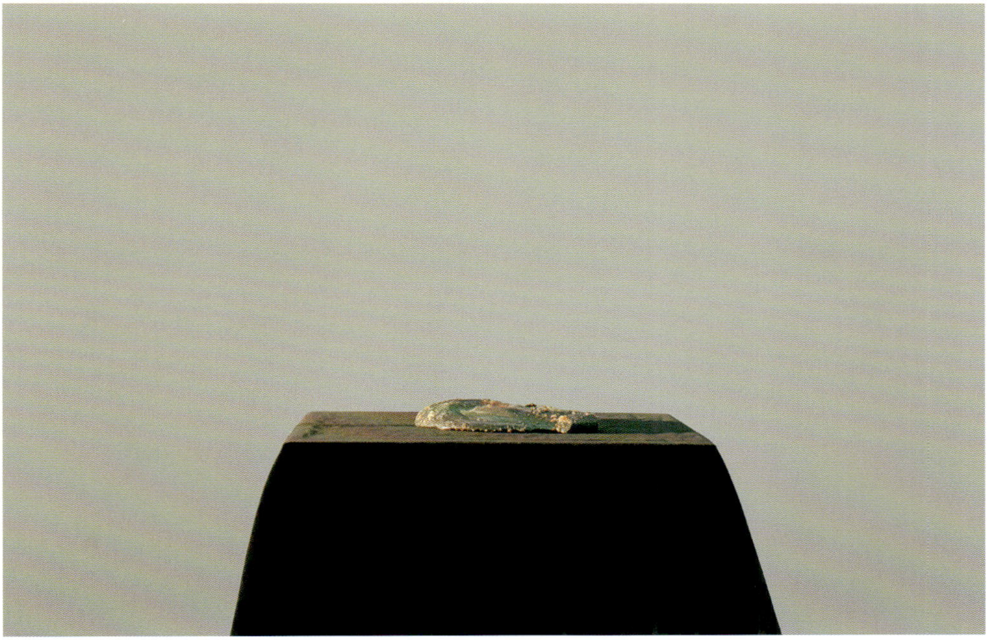

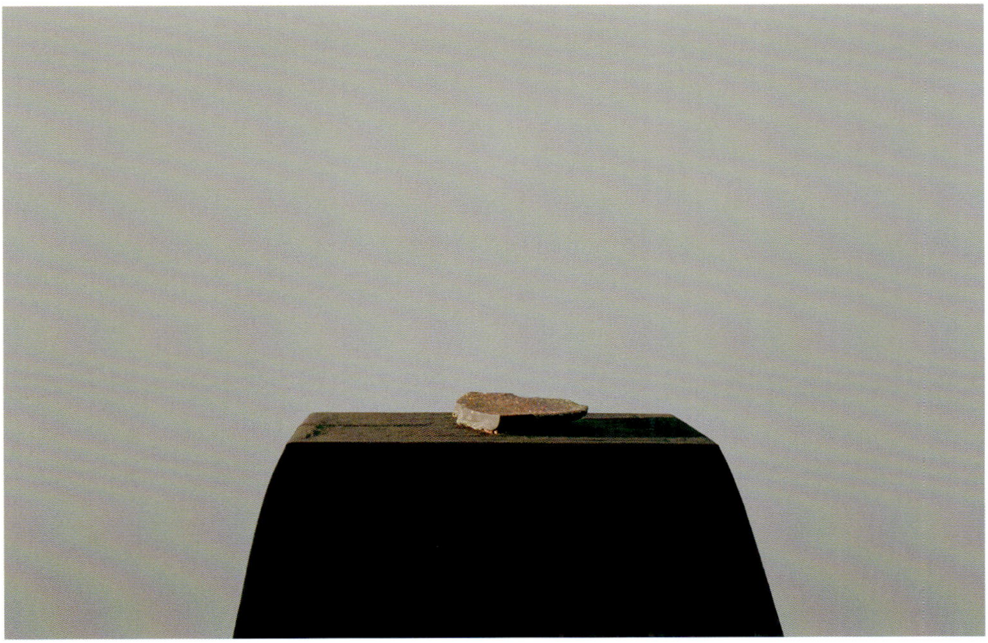

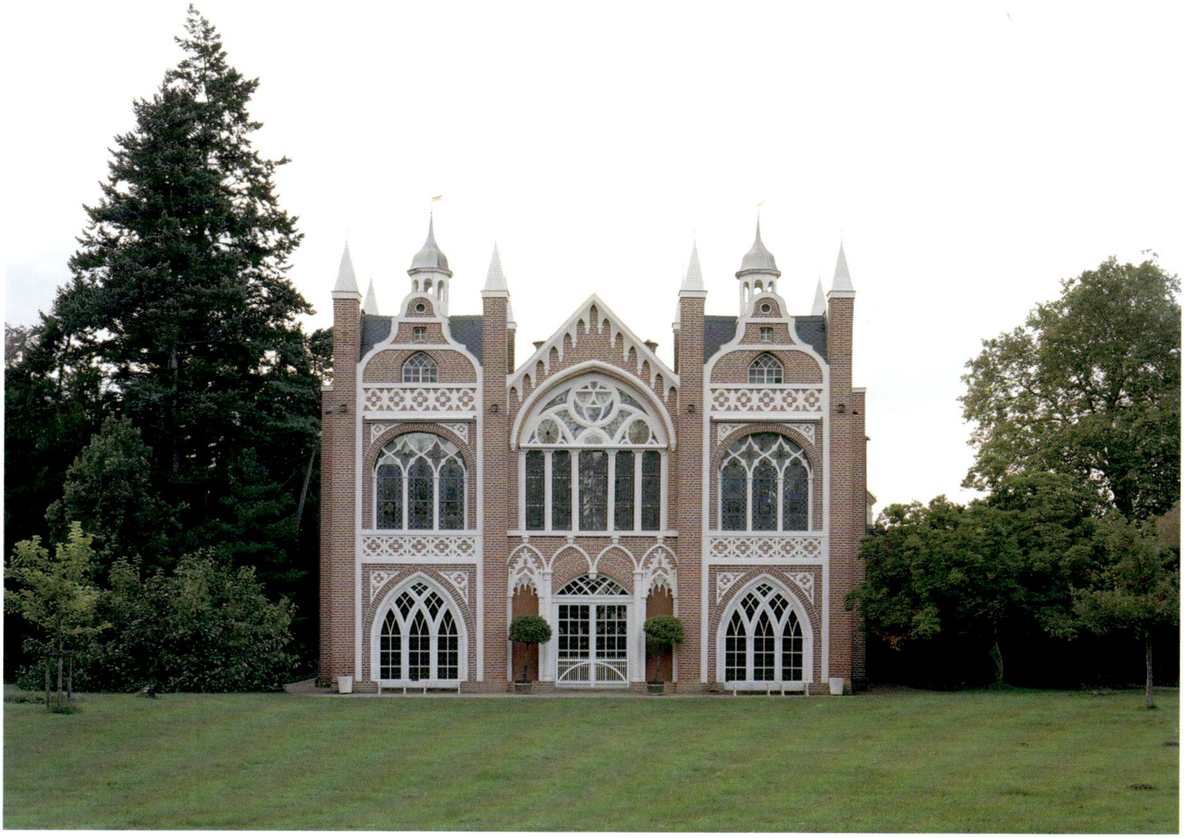

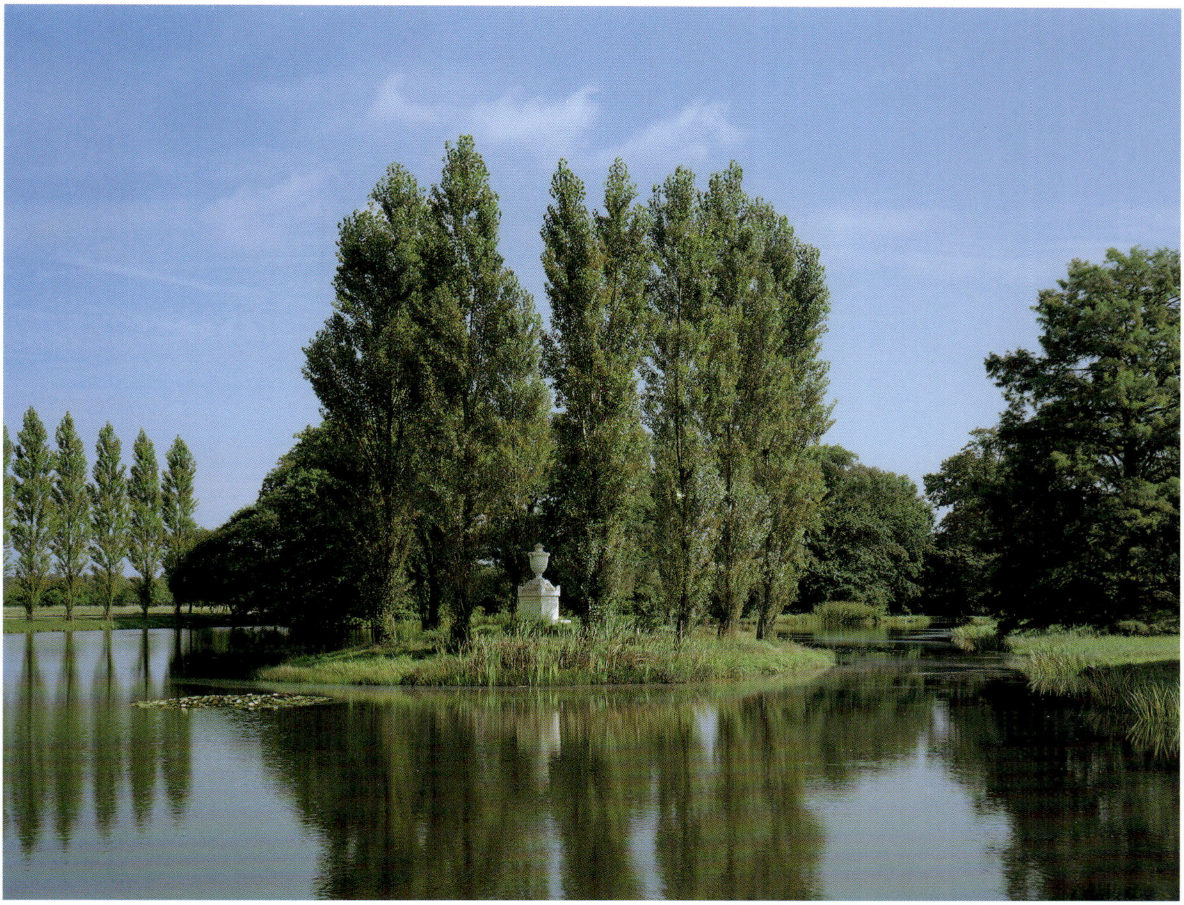

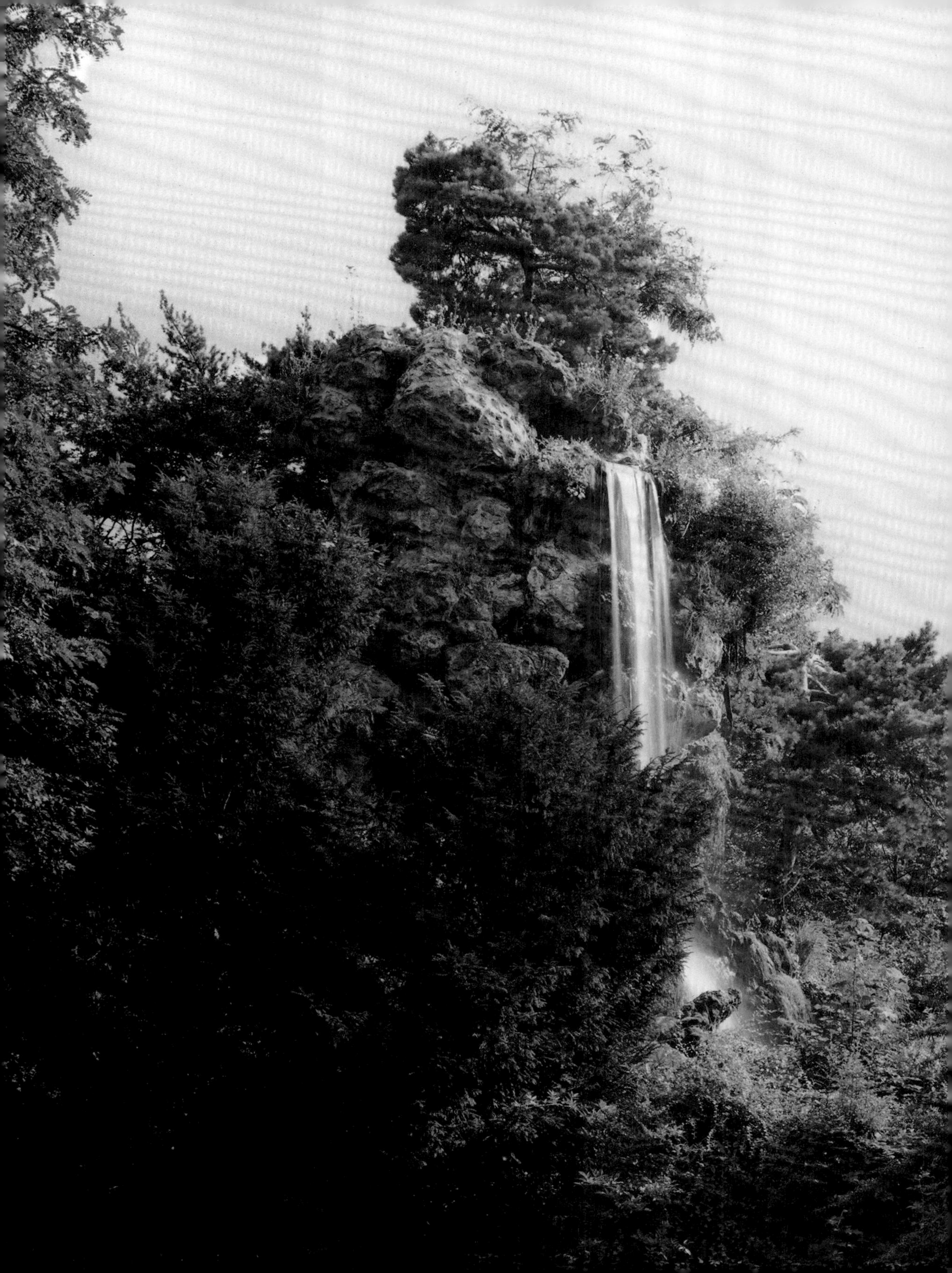

To be loved to be told—*Hark, it's His Royal Highness*, and when you are loved you want more love
you want more
love

Next room.

Overlooking where you have been. Those people below having original experiences.

A puddle of spilt *Trapeze* and broken glass.

Likewise characterised as a Community Leader when—ghoulish tremors—teacher, classmate, lover—you see The Three Exes.

We have a situation.

'Lawrence Weiner' wearing a GHOST STORIES T-shirt and it could be deliberate you are aware of multiple roles.

Live dangerously?

I want to see.

Say what? says the waiter.

What is it you want to see? whispers the wind in the voice of your Guru

Try picturing that baby's face.

Next room.

tick tick tick tick
Back where you started.

Hello Gruesome, says Bad Breakup, looming with a demonic smile.

Must this be done, now and here?

Live dangerously?

As it really is him, will you break character?

Woof! Woof!

Recruitment Development Consultant

Woof! Woof!

Practice Support Analyst

Woof! Woof!

Policy Safeguarding Executive

Woof! Woof!

Client Delivery Fundraiser

Woof! Woof!

Bad Breakup laughs—*You always were barking mad.*

GHOST STORIES

phibrations

Live dangerously?

You need a drink.

Tapioca Tea Trapeze, the waiter says. *Threat level moderate.*

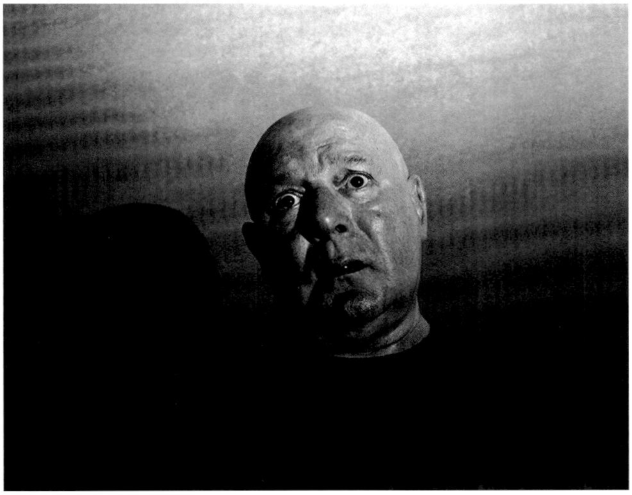

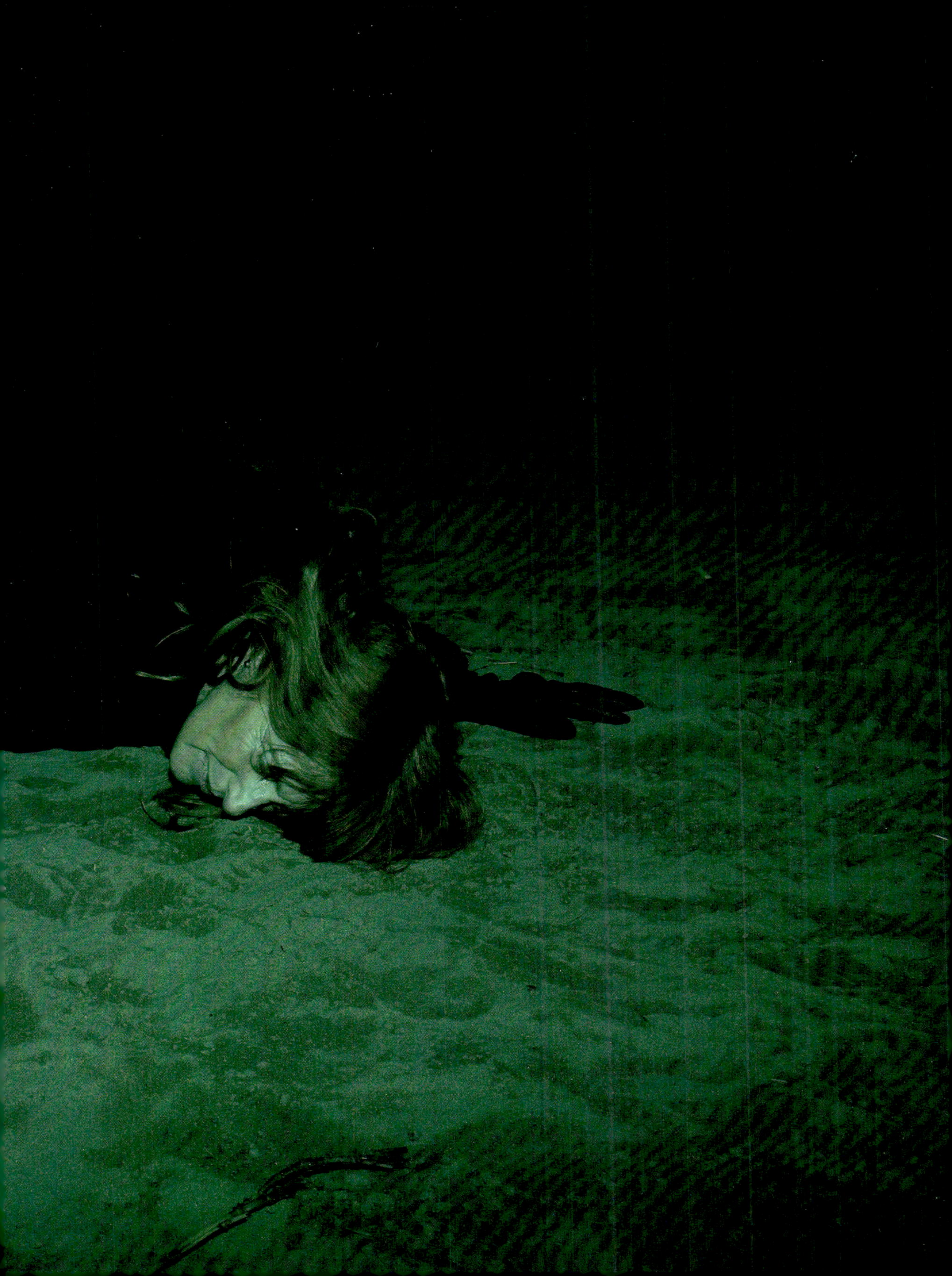

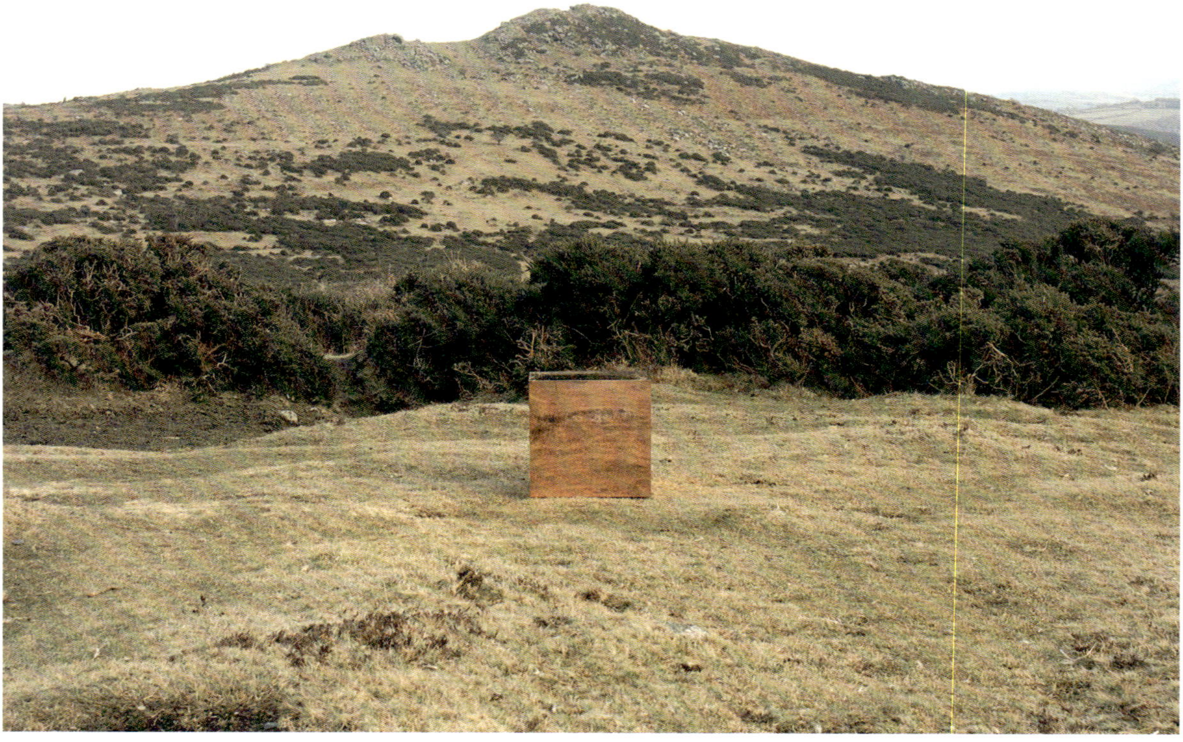

Down it. Escape. Bad Breakup follows.

We need to talk.

Where is your Guru?

Shame.

boom—they pound at the door—the door swells and, as if by the hand of a devious ghost, the chain unravels...

tick tick tick tick

The door opens partially—only the padlock holding it closed.

Naked and grasping arms reach in.

We never did really finish things properly.

Girl—*If you want out, just say.*
Boy—*I don't know what I want.*

Enter Chris Martin.

bang

A drum strapped to his back.

bang

Turn and run.

bang

Collide with a waiter.

bang

Trapeze everywhere.

bang

The padlock breaks—doors open—a gust of wind and pause—face off with the braying mob—silence.

Chris Martin sings—*For a second I was in control, I had it once, I lost it though.*

He bangs his drum. The three-piece band seen earlier are his bandmates from Coldplay. They join the song, accompanied by the drumbeats and whistles of the protestors.

The waiter takes off his shirt and dances. Clouds from smoke bombs cushion the light. Security, 'Lawrence Weiner', the Official Photographer, everyone is there, arms aloft. Phil reunited with his group and the arguing couple kissing. Through the clouds, your Guru reappears, smiling—*Feel good?* He puts his arm around you.

Chris Martin sings—*Just tell me you love me, if you don't then lie.*

GHOST STORIES
by Paul Haworth

Paul Haworth (Lancaster, 1982)
is an artist working with words and performance.
He lives in London.

List of Works

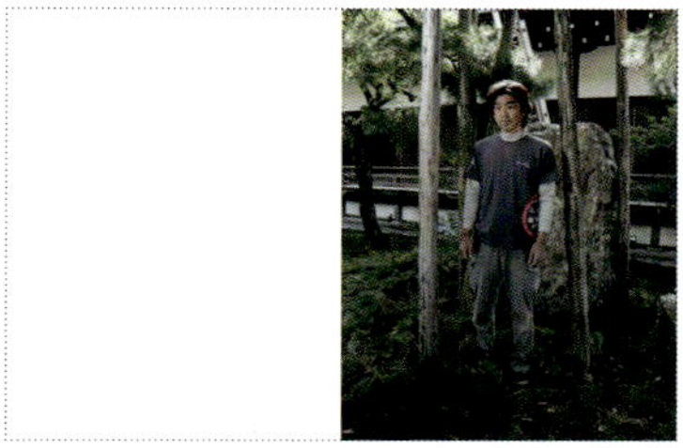

1

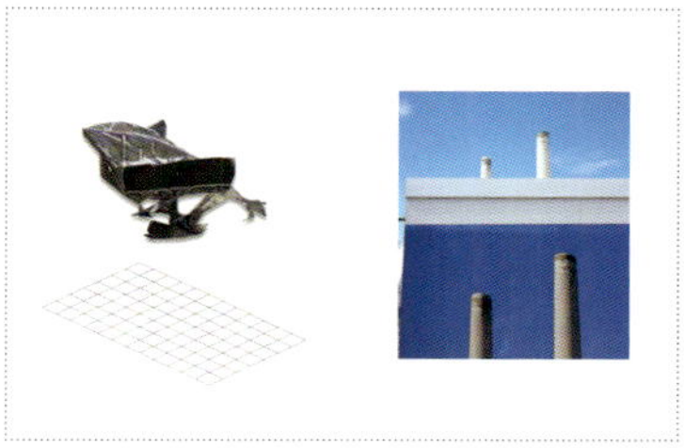

8 9

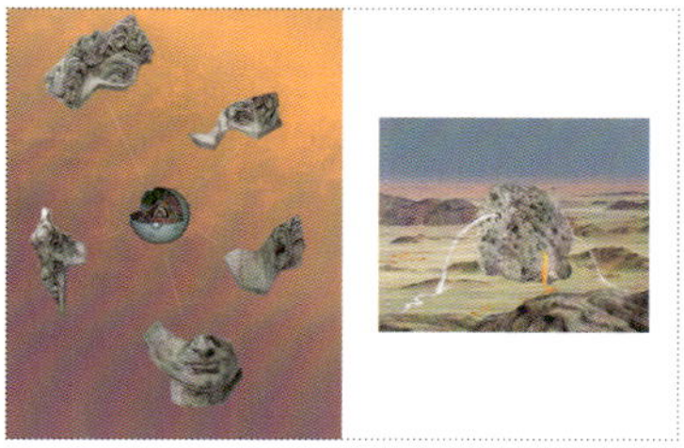

10 11

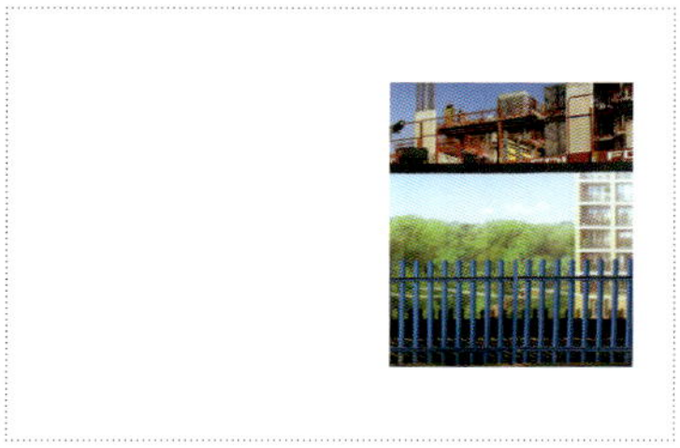

13

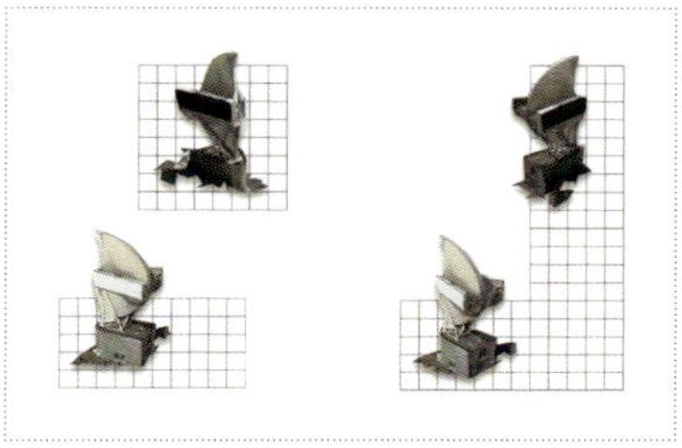

14 15

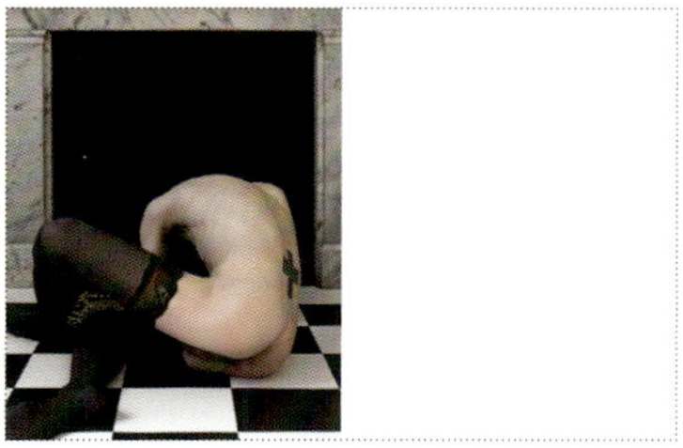

16

18 19

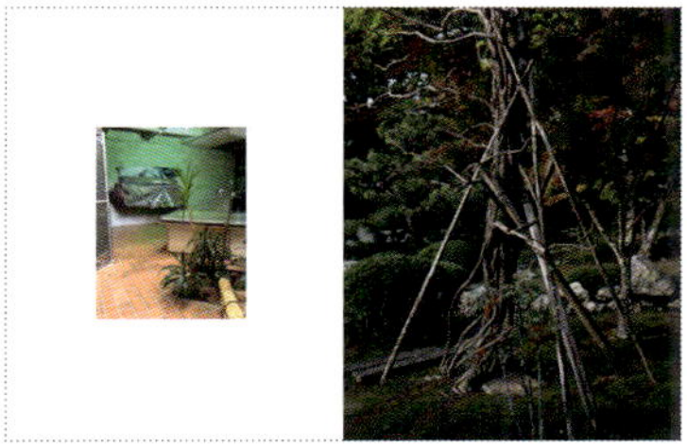

20 21

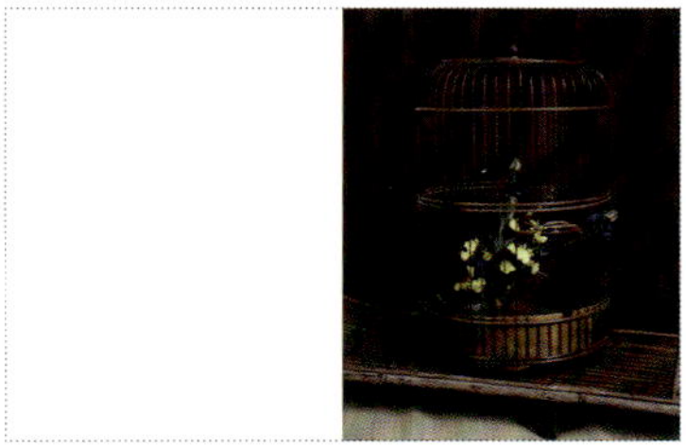

25

1 **Carlos Jiménez**
Master Gardener 1
carlos-jimenez.com

8 **Benjamin Cosmo Westoby**
mining virtuality_ excavation_ I.I
benwestoby.com

9 **Alexander Christie**
The greatest transformational story
alexanderchristie.co.uk

10 **Alis Oldfield**
Where No Man Has Gone Before
alisoldfield.co.uk

11 **Alis Oldfield**
The Way to Eden
alisoldfield.co.uk

13 **Alexander Christie**
Lakeview… the next chapter
alexanderchristie.co.uk

14 **Benjamin Cosmo Westoby**
mining virtuality_ excavation_I.II
benwestoby.com

15 **Benjamin Cosmo Westoby**
mining virtuality_ excavation_I.IV
benwestoby.com

16 **Philomene Hoel**
philomenehoel.fr

18-20 **Bláithín Mac Donnell**
blaithinmacdonnell.com

21 **Carlos Jiménez**
Tree House 1
carlos-jimenez.com

25 **Carlos Jiménez**
Flower House 1
carlos-jimenez.com

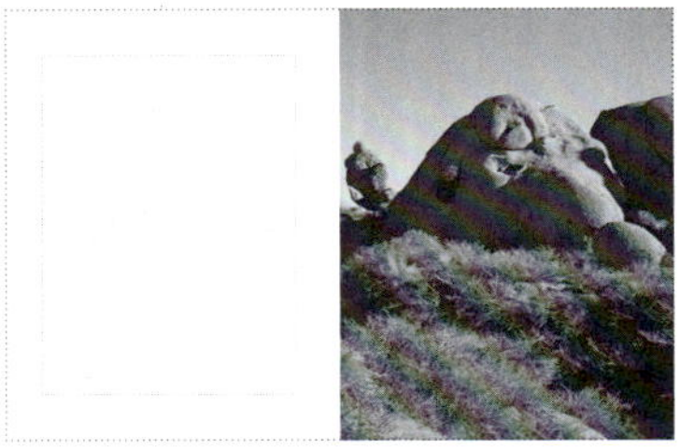

26 27

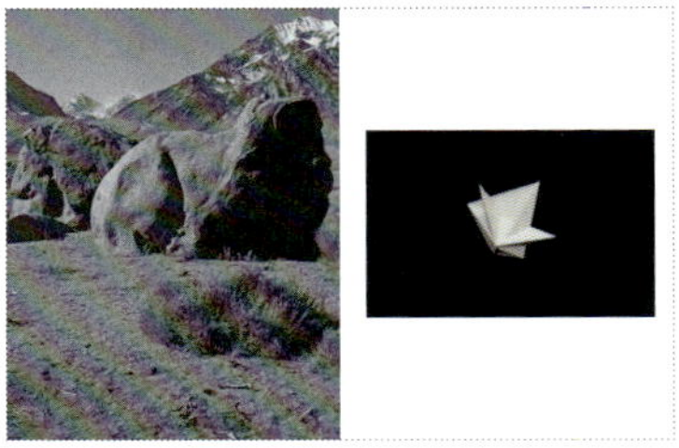

28 29

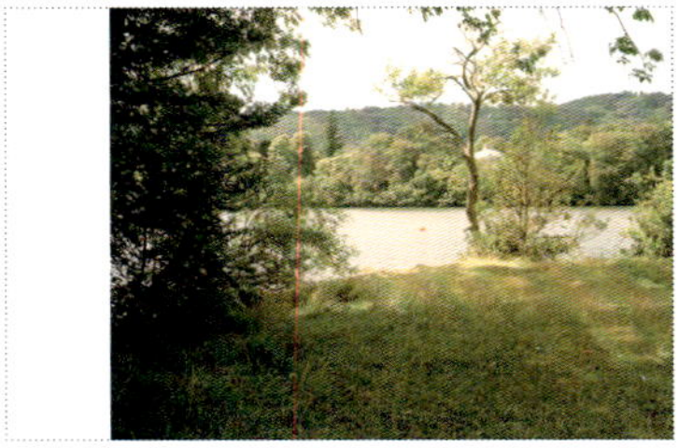

30

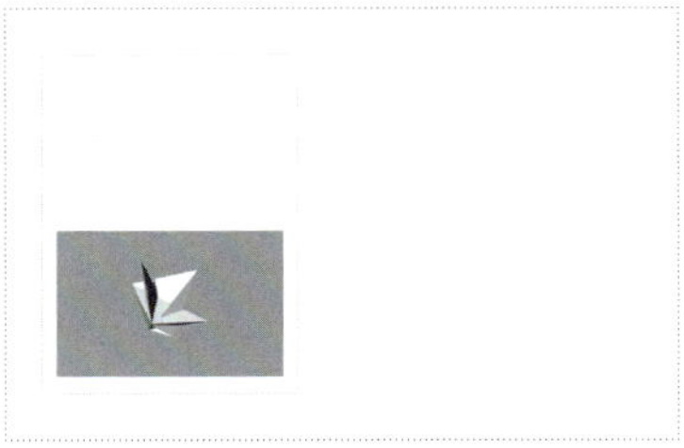

32

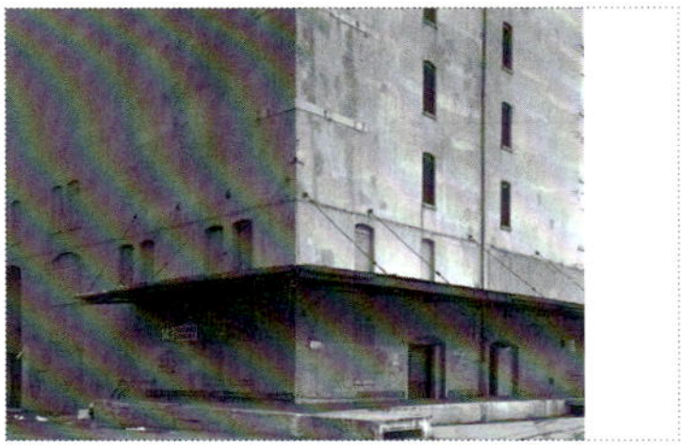

34

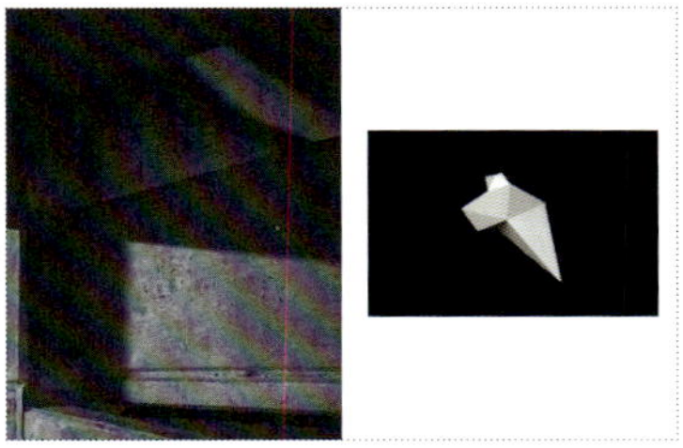

36 37

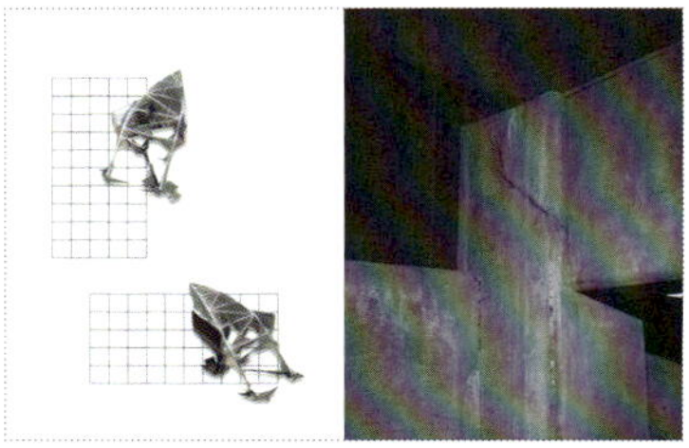

38 39

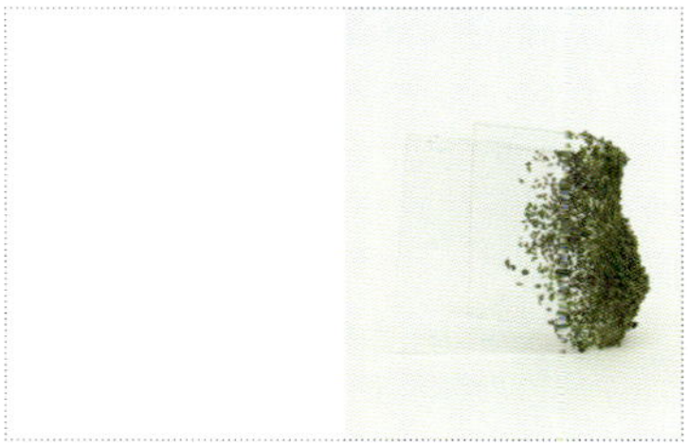

41

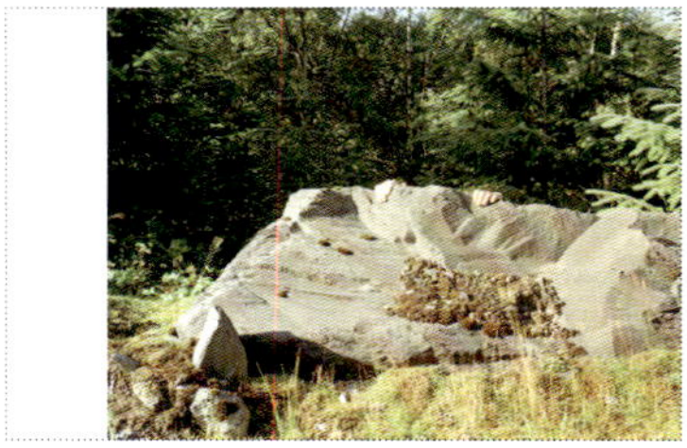

42

26-28 **Erin Solomons**
erinsolomons.com

29 **JiangYin Qu**
jiangyin.qu@network.
rca.ac.uk

30 **Feiyi Wen**
wenfeiyi.com

32 **JiangYin Qu**
jiangyin.qu@network.
rca.ac.uk

34-36 **Hanqing Ma**
in collaboration with
Mona H Yoo
The Exit Strategy
hanqingphoto.com
mona-h-yoo.com

37 **JiangYin Qu**
jiangyin.qu@network.
rca.ac.uk

38 Benjamin Cosmo Westoby
*mining virtuality_*
excavation_I.III
benwestoby.com

39 **Hanqing Ma in**
collaboration with
Mona H Yoo
The Exit Strategy
hanqingphoto.com
mona-h-yoo.com

41 **Liam Tickner**
A round-trip journey to
Mars is no picnic
liamtickner.com

42 **Feiyi Wen**
wenfeiyi.com

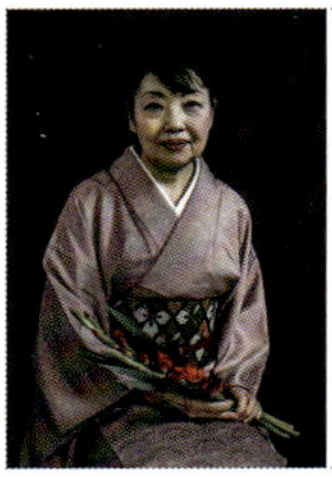

44

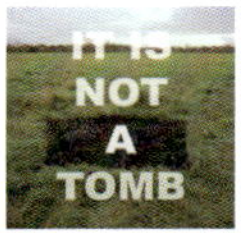

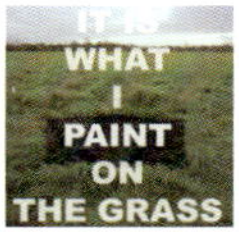

48 49

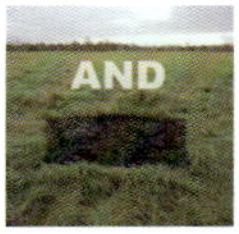

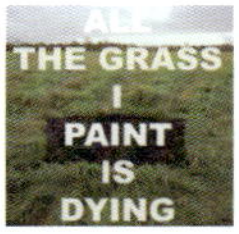

50 51

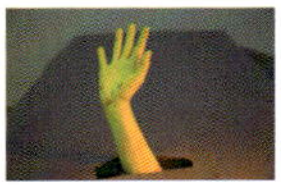

53

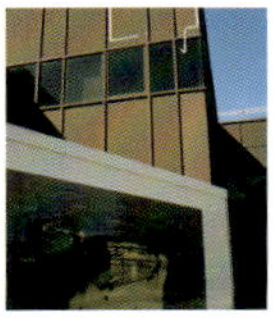

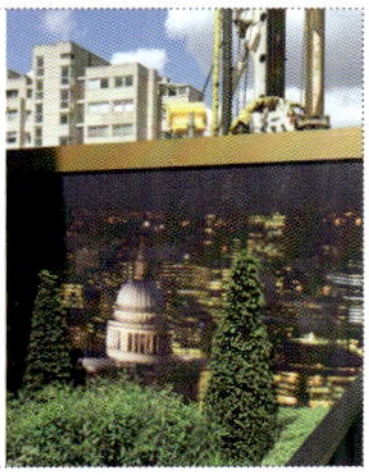

54 55

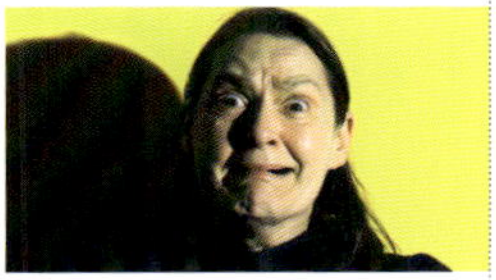

56

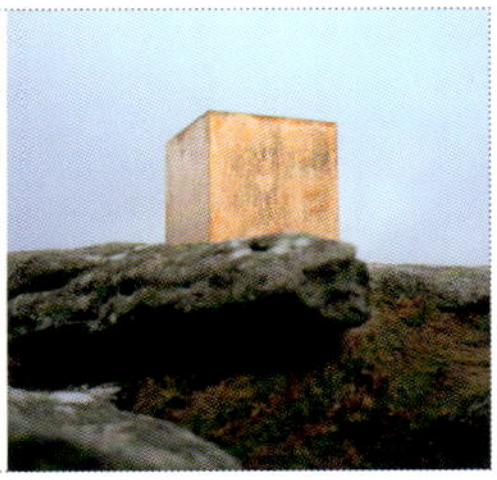

58

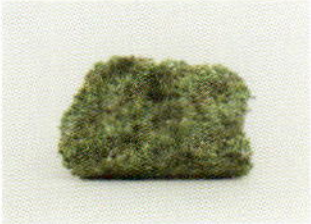

60

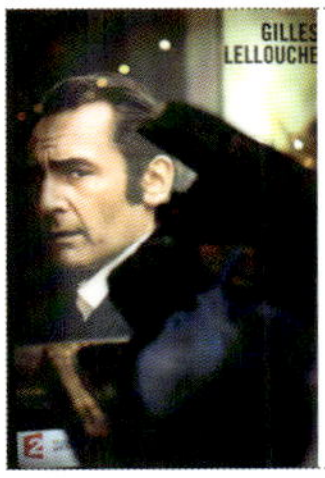

62

44 **Carlos Jiménez**
Master Ikebana
carlos-jimenez.com

48-51 **Jin Li**
jin.li@network.rca.ac.uk

53 **Louise Fitzgerald**
Create a person
louise-fitzgerald.com

54 **Alexander Christie**
Live Original
alexanderchristie.co.uk

55 **Alexander Christie**
In Lieu
alexanderchristie.co.uk

56 **Kristen Abdai**
kristenabdai.net

58 **Julie Cai**
jia.cai@network.rca.ac.uk

60 **Liam Tickner**
A round-trip journey to Mars is no picnic
liamtickner.com

62 **Ruidi Mu**
Down and out in Paris
ruidi.mu@network.rca.ac.uk

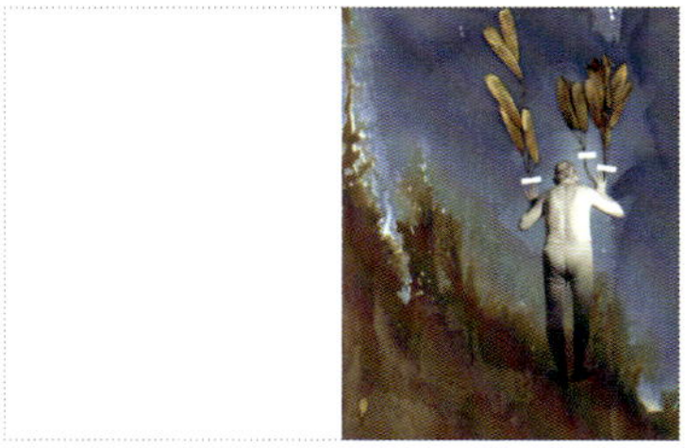

67

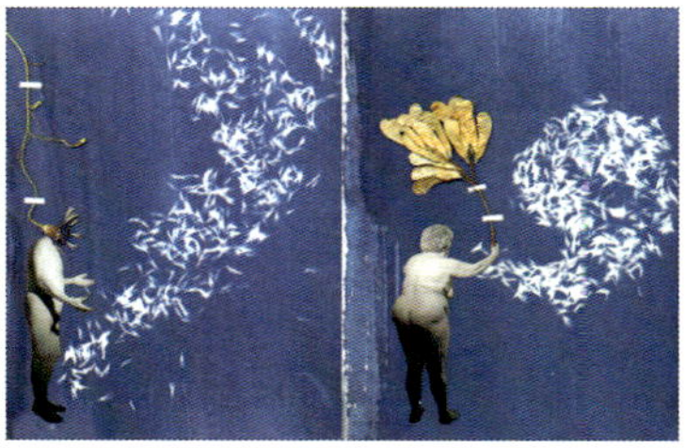

68 69

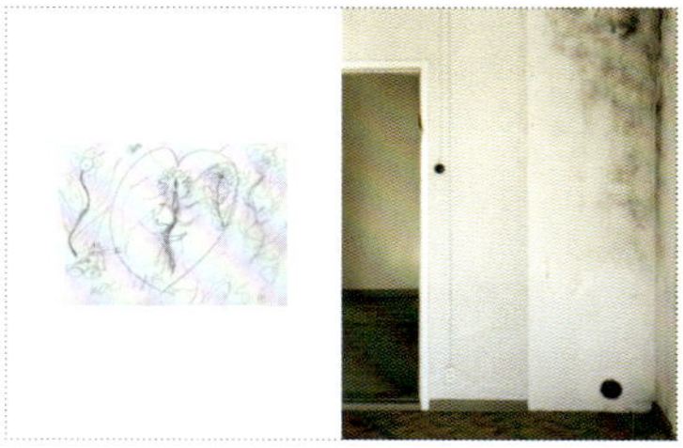

70 71

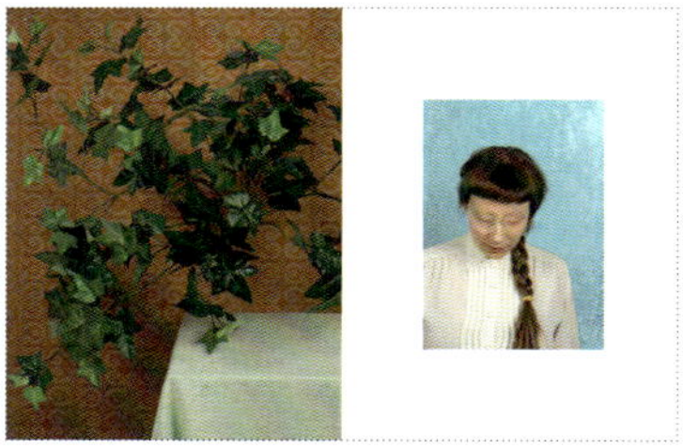

72 73

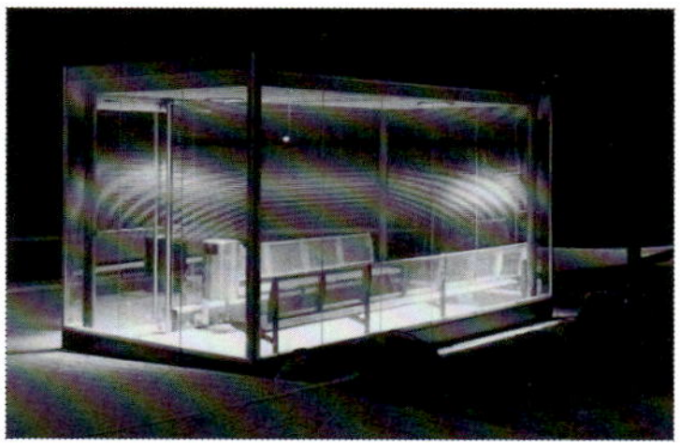

74

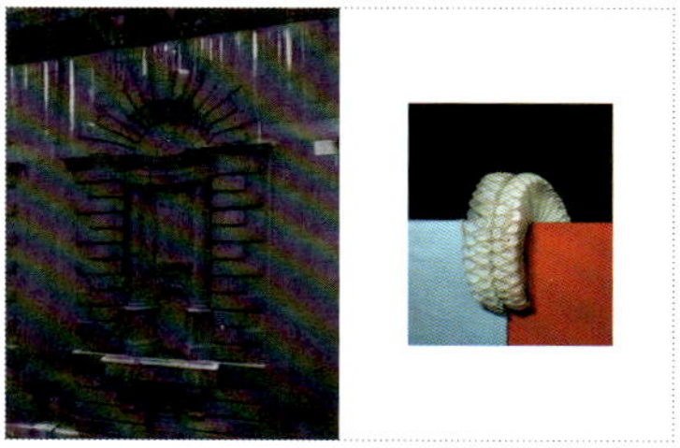

76 77

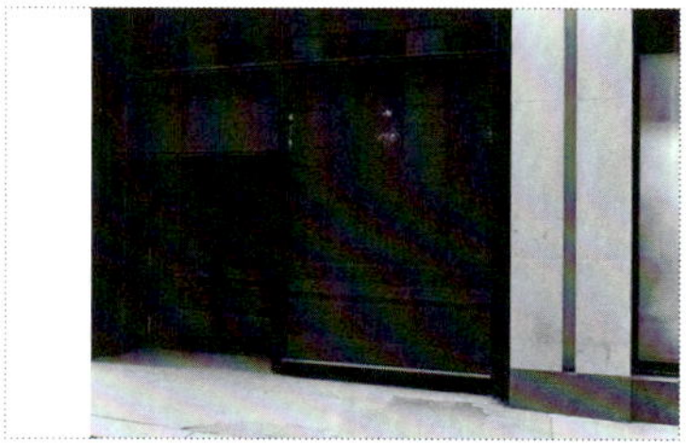

78

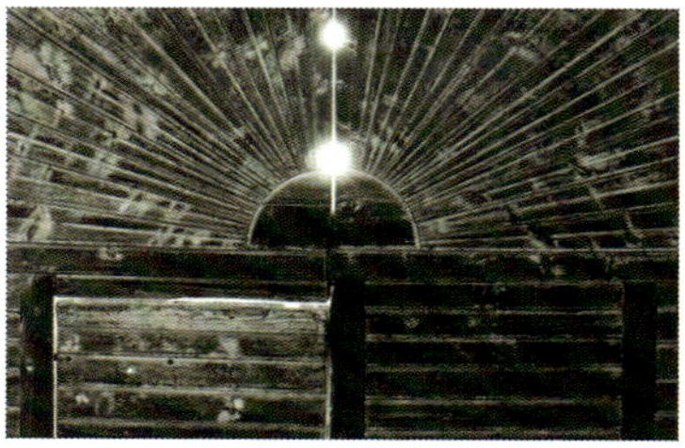

82

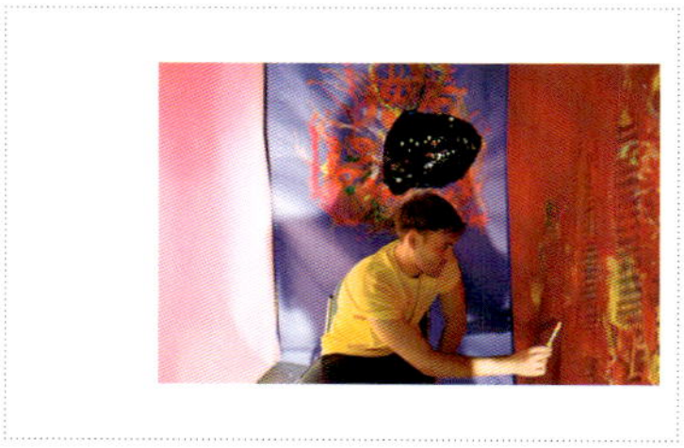

84

67 **Maja A Ngom**
Herbarium, Fragment #2
maja-absa.ngom@network.rca.ac.u
majaangom.com

68 **Maja A Ngom**
Herbarium, Fragment #1
maja-absa.ngom@network.rca.ac.u
majaangom.com

69 **Maja A Ngom**
Herbarium, Fragment #3
maja-absa.ngom@network.rca.ac.u
majaangom.com

70 **Ruidi Mu**
Down and out in Paris
ruidi.mu@network.rca.ac.uk

71-73
Martina Lindqvist
martinalindqvist.com

74 **Matan Ashkenazy**
Railway Station 2015
matan.ashkenazy@network.rca.ac.uk

76 **Matan Ashkenazy**
Façade A 2015
matan.ashkenazy@network.rca.ac.uk

77 **Philomene Hoel**
philomenehoel.fr

78 **Matan Ashkenazy**
matan.ashkenazy@network.rca.ac.uk

82 **Silje Lovise Gjertsen**
The Moon Rise
siljelovise.com

84 **Louise Fitzgerald**
louise-fitzgerald.com

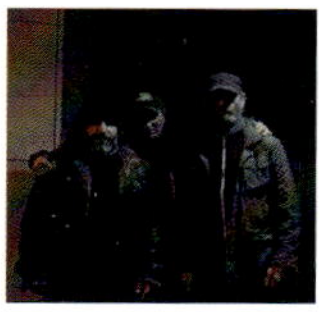

87

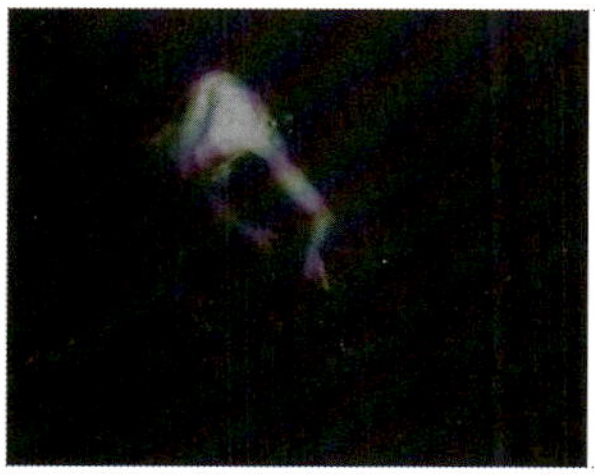

88

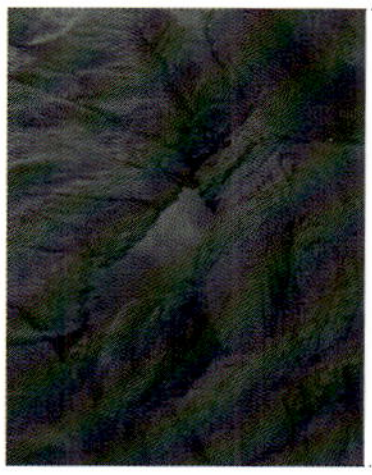

90

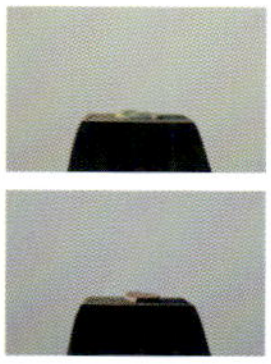

91

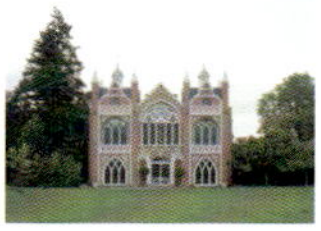

92

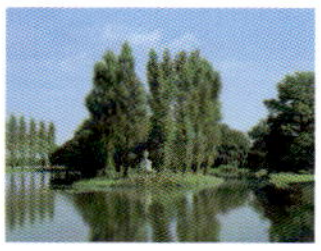

93

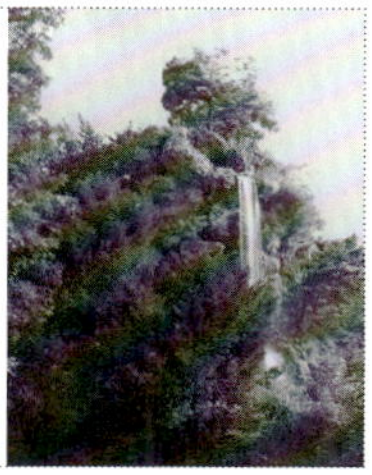

95

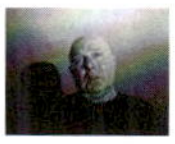

97

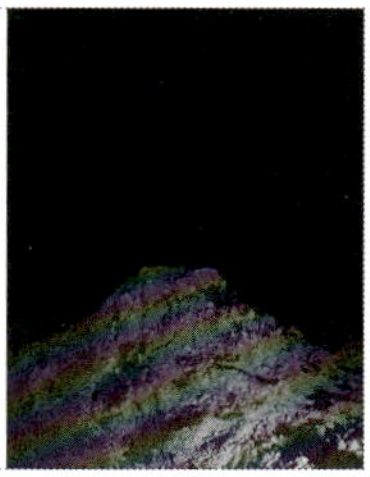

99

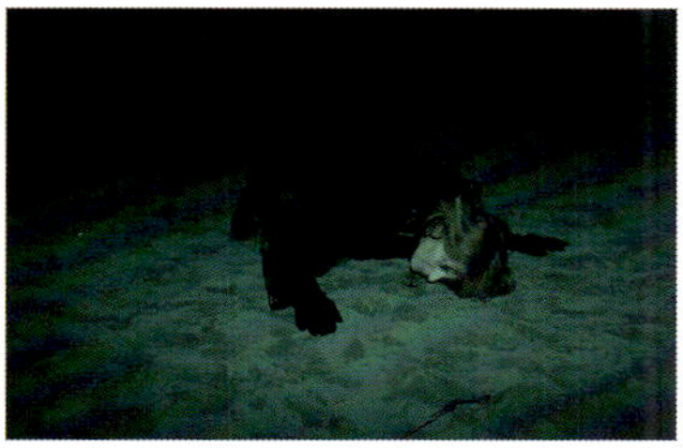

100

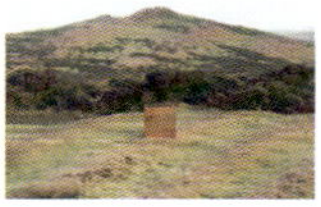

102

87 **Ruidi Mu**
Down and out in Paris
ruidi.mu@network.rca.ac.uk

88 **Silje Lovise Gjertsen**
The Fall
siljelovise.com

90 **Silje Lovise Gjertsen**
The Mind is a Portal
siljelovise.com

91 **Yu-Chien Chien**
yuchien.chien@network.
rca.ac.uk

92-95 **Sophie Neilson**
sophieneilson.com

97 **Kristen Abdai**
kristenabdai.net

99-100 **Tanya Moulson**
News from Nowhere
tanyamoulson.com

102 **Julie Cai**
jia.cai@network.rca.ac.uk

End-Troduction

A conversation between Alis Oldfield, Benjamin Cosmo Westoby & Rut Blees Luxemburg

AO ... but the present can't exist. There is no single time of the present, its total mass—the current moment of say, some seven billion people, is beyond all possible experience. It exists only for a moment and all separately and yet we talk about the present, the contemporary, as a whole, as a set thing. The present is actually speculative.

RBL So why are you so interested in the contemporary?

AO I think that this idea of accepting and getting lost in fictions, is of the now.

RBL But isn't the contemporary always of the now?

AO Of course but the idea of immersive absorption, of losing yourself, is particular to this now! Maybe we're trying to escape the hyper cool self-consciousness of Postmodernism and in doing so we've retreated into something that's more light or escapist.

RBL What do you think this has to do with the book?

AO I think that it has to do with photography in that the photograph takes something temporal and elongates the space. It creates something alternate that you can enter into.

BCW Also this idea of the space between the future and the past, what the present does, it's this space of regurgitation where things travel through it like a conduit. Which is perhaps an interesting way of looking at image making.

AO Yes precisely, it's fake but it's also entirely real. Photography has the ability to fictionalise our reality by reproducing it.

BCW It's funny, but there is something interesting in this idea—I don't know—the failure to sum things up. Or to try to consolidate everything into something that means something. It's an absurd thing to try to achieve.

AO Especially with this idea of the contemporary, this amalgamation of all human experience happening all at once—it's so intangible.

BCW People often feel a need to make connections between things, for there to be a sense of reassurance in trying to quantify things and create relationships with them. So in a way, trying to make a publication like this one is trying to draw impossible associations between things.

RBL But why, why would it be impossible—we've just done it perhaps?

BCW Yeah but you've just said it was a failure! Maybe it wasn't possible.

RBL It's not 100 per cent a failure, it's only 50 per cent a failure!

RBL What makes me kind of uneasy is that I detect a certain type of nihilism.

AO Well, we are Generation Y anyway, aren't we. We were brought up on things like *The Simpsons*—we're inherently nihilistic! We retreat into video games or worlds that take you out of the real—we're not trying to fix our own reality, we're trying to escape it, trying to find a strategy for existence.

BCW ... I guess it's funny as we were one of the first generations that had this experience of not having the internet and being aware of not having it. Children now have screens from the moment that they are born pretty much.

AO And we're sceptical of it as well, I think, because of that. Part of us wants to get lost in these places but there's a cynicism there as well, we know it's a surrogate or a substitute, perhaps.

RBL Now we're not going to make this just about your generation—we have to find a further angle. How can this go beyond your understanding of who you think you are?

RBL Do you think that a publication as a platform is still important?

AO That's a big question, Christ!

BCW What is it contributing do you mean? I suppose that now you are competing with these spaces (points at laptop), with screens, that offer different possibilities. I guess they capture your attention in a different way—I don't know. Very seductive things happen through the screen. Everything seems to be converted into binaries through these new channels. The book has this inertness that makes it quiet somehow—it requires something from the person viewing it.

RBL Isn't the book actually more free, don't you think—more private than what you have on the screen? The old fashioned book is more covert—there is something more secret and hence more powerful too, *being under the radar*...

AO Maybe the difficulty lies in being an 'anti-rebel'—being sincere, actually having a position and believing in something.

RBL ... and of course, its unalterable. What's in the book—how we have laid it out, how we have edited it—will be the same in ten years time. So it really will be a document and a record of a position, whereas everything on the screen is in constant flux. There is no past, or future—maybe this is your constant presence, your constant contemporary.

AO And we're asking someone to forget that mode of escape, to instead explore something constant yet ambiguous. Perhaps it serves as an antidote—to willingly suspend your disbelief and become immersed, in spite of yourself....

Immanuel Kant tells us that "the delight which determines the judgement of taste is independent of all interests". And also: "one must not be in the least prepossessed in favour of the real existence of the thing, but must preserve complete indifference in this respect in order to play the part of judge in matters of taste". The judgement of taste is determined by the feeling of pleasure or displeasure. It is the way in which I am affected by a representation. The aesthetic, in its simpler form, is the contemplation of "a representation with an accompanying sensation of delight". It points to the difference between pleasure and desire. My aesthetic pleasure is dependent upon my absence of desire for what is being represented, and nothing "should make me dependent on the real existence of the object". Isn't there a disavowal at work there? I know that the judgement of taste is disinterested, and yet taste as sensation is not. Is there a suspension of disbelief here, as I must do as if I am disinterested? Isn't there an oscillation between taste as a judgement predicated upon distance and indifference, and taste as an incorporation and assimilation of the object into my body?

For Ernst Gombrich, "food is the first thing on which we train our critical faculties from the moment of birth. The very word taste which we use to describe a person's aesthetic responses suggests this model. But so strong is the Platonic prejudice in favour of the spiritual senses, the eye and the ear, that a blanket of social disapproval seems still to cover such animal gratification as eating and drinking." Looking is associated with eating, and "indeed some paintings are made for the dining room—a feast for the eye". Taste as a sense impression and the aesthetic judgement of taste are not clearly separated, as the former may inform the latter. When looking at pictures as a form of tasting, he proposes to make a difference between the soft and the crunchy. What is too sweet, too syrupy, too sugary, too milky, too fat is welcomed by the child. It is rejected by the sophisticated adult who seeks a more bitter tang, as in coffee and crunchy nuts. The articulation between soft and crunchy is from Edward Glover, in "The Significance of the Mouth in Psychoanalysis", 1924. The analyst writes: "study the mouthpiece of pipes, the stub ends of pencils… observe the degree of partial incorporation of the soup spoon." It is as if signs of incorporation have left marks, as reminders that the acts of licking, sucking and biting are part of the everyday. Biting and sucking are gratifications which are part of our daily life.

Michel Onfray, in *Le Ventre des Philosophes* (The Belly of the Philosophers) is interested in Kant's taste for taste. There are not many examples of food in *The Critique of Judgement*. Kant mentions wine from the Canary Islands as an example of a judgement of the senses. To say that Canary wine is good, is merely a subjective judgement: it is good for me. The pleasure provided by spicy food is an example of something which is not good in itself, as the temporary pleasure it provides may be followed by a perturbed digestion. The judgement of taste proper may begin when our desire for food has been fulfilled. It may begin when need or desire are absent. Kant places taste and smell as belonging to the lower senses. They are spiritually lower, because they are closer to the body. With taste, something enters my palate and saliva dissolves it into my body. With smell, something enters my organism through my nose. In both cases, something has crossed the boundary between the external world and the body. The lower senses are those that enter the subject. They are inescapably subjective. Smell would be the lowest of the low in this case. I am unable to refuse a smell, especially a bad smell, as it enters my organism and becomes part of me, against my will. In this respect, smell is contrary to elementary freedom. Taste at least involves choice. I can spit out bad food. How can I sniff out a bad smell? Yet taste remains fully on the side of the subjective. It is irrevocably relative and particular to the taster, and Kant is not very interested in theorising the particular. The higher senses are sight and hearing because they involve a distance between me and the object. Touch is in between, it is more immediate, as there is contact with the object. Sight and hearing are more objective, they involve a distance between the subject and the object, a distance that the lower senses irrevocably dissolve. The higher senses are thought to be purer as there is a mediation between the subject and the object, and the object remains outside of ourselves.

When in his 30s, Kant drank so much in one of the inns of Königsberg that he could hardly find his way home. He does offer an analysis of being drunk, and notes the different effects of beer, wine and spirits upon the mind. Drunkenness, from a moral point of view belongs to the good, as it encourages a quality: frankness. Kant is normally a model of moderation. He would drink wine, never beer, a drink he held responsible for haemorrhoids and mortality. Kant took his breakfast at 5 o'clock in the morning, with two cups of tea. He never ate alone at lunch time because eating is a sociable activity. For lunch, he had three different dishes, one of his favourite being cod, followed by cheese with butter. Late in his life when food had to be cut for him on his plate, the philosopher scolded his servant, who had prepared his meal too coarsely. Kant had asked for a better sense of form on his plate.

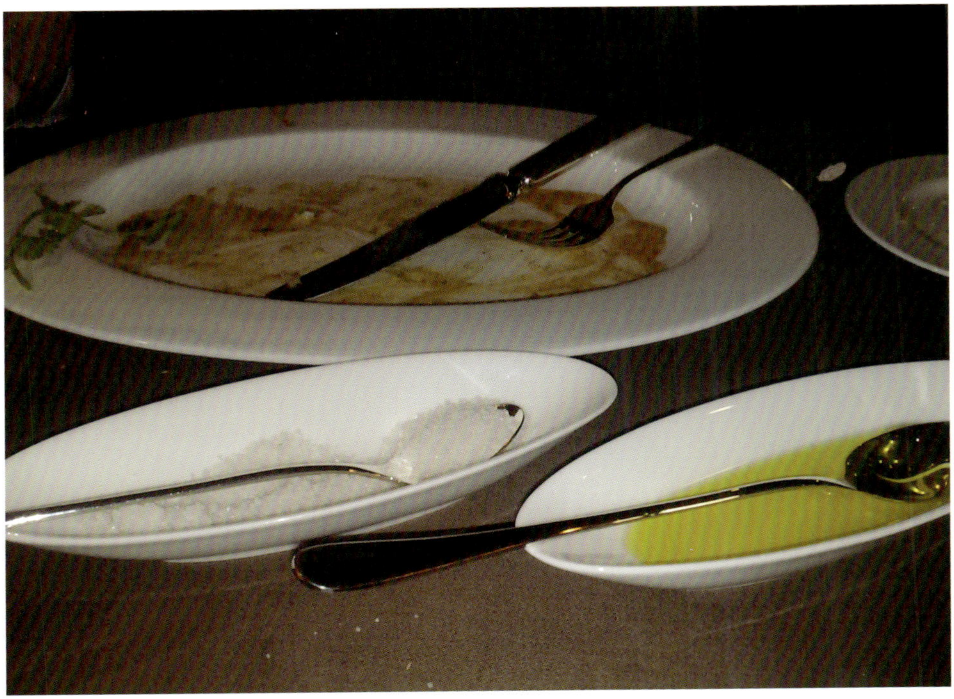

Edward Glover, "The Significance of the Mouth in Psycho-Analysis", 1924
Ernst Gombrich, "Psycho-Analysis and the History of Art", 1953
Immanuel Kant, *Critique of Judgement*, 1790
Michel Onfray, *Le Ventre des Philosophes*, 1989

Thanks to the
Photography Programme, RCA.

Black Dog Publishing Limited
10a Acton Street
London WC1X 9NG
United Kingdom

Tel: +44(0)20 7713 5097
Fax: +44 (0)20 7713 8682
info@blackdogonline.com
www.blackdogonline.com

ISBN 978 1 910433 10 2
British Library Cataloguing-in-Publication
Data. A CIP record for this book is available
from the British Library.

Black Dog Publishing Limited, London, UK,
is an environmentally responsible company.
Exit Strategies is printed on a sustainably
sourced paper.

Edited by
Rut Blees Luxemburg

Editorial team,
Alis Oldfield
Benjamin Cosmo Westoby
Katherine Reynolds

Designed by
Carole Courtillé
Mads Freund Brunse

Front cover: Carlos Jiménez
Back cover: Tanya Moulson

Exit Strategies follows on from
Science & Fiction, ISBN 978 1 908966 50 6
Waving Flags, ISBN 978 1 908966 10 0
Seeing for Others, ISBN 978 1 907317 62 0
Hardcover: Image Perspectives,
ISBN 978 1 907317 41 5
previous titles published in a
collaboration between
Black Dog Publishing Limited and
The Royal College of Art's MA
Photography Programme.

In association with
Royal College of Art
Dyson Building, 20 Howie Street
London SW11 4AS
United Kingdom
rca.ac.uk

Royal College of Art
Postgraduate Art & Design

reuse recycle reduce

architecture art design
fashion history photography
theory and things
www.blackdogonline.com

black dog publishing
london uk